CW00350822

Acknowledgements

The author would like to express his gratitude to the Trustees of the P. G. Wodehouse Estate for permission to quote so freely from the Wodehouse works. He would also like to thank Sir Edward Cazalet for his generous support and Anthony Whittome of Hutchinson, Random House for good advice. The author and publishers are grateful to David Higham Associates for permission to quote from *Like It Was* by Malcolm Muggeridge, published by HarperCollins.

Every effort has been made to trace the copyright holders of material quoted herein. The publishers would be pleased to hear from any we have been unable to contact in order to rectify any omissions in future editions.

Mark Hichens is deeply indebted, of course, to Wendy McLerie for her excellent drawings, which have added a new dimension to the book, and would like to congratulate all at Book Guild on the production of the book.

P. G. Wodehouse
The Story of His Life

THE INIMITABLE P. G. WODEHOUSE

By the same author

Wives of the Kings of England: From Normans to Stuarts

Wives of the Kings of England: From Hanover to Windsor

Prime Ministers' Wives

Oscar Wilde's Last Chance: The Dreyfus Connection

West Downs: A Portrait of an English Prep School

The Troubled Century: British and World History, 1914–93

THE INIMITABLE
P. G. WODEHOUSE

The Story of His Life and A Treasury of His Wit

Mark Hichens

Illustrations by Wendy McLerie

Book Guild Publishing
Sussex, England

First published in Great Britain in 2009 by
The Book Guild Ltd
Pavilion View
Brighton, BN1 1UF

Typeset in Garamond by
Ellipsis Books Limited, Glasgow

Printed in Great Britain by
CPI Antony Rowe

A catalogue record for this book is available from
The British Library.

ISBN 978 1 84624 334 9

Contents

Preface

To add to the existing works on P. G. Wodehouse needs, surely, a word of explanation. The author is aware of how many of these there are already, including full-length biographies, detailed studies, as well as such Wodehouse byways as those on the exact location of Market Blandings and the drinking habits of Bertie Wooster. It might well be thought that the subject of P. G. Wodehouse has been exhausted; but it is a rich territory, and it is likely that there will be prospectors there yet.

The limitations of the present book should be stated at once: it is not making use of newly discovered material; it is not upsetting all previous estimates of Wodehouse, the man and the writer; and it is not making an analytical study of his humour. The book consists of two parts: a brief biography and a treasury of memorable quotations; and each, it is claimed, has a new angle. The biography is not only more compact than its predecessors, but also makes more extensive use of Wodehouse's works of fiction. There was much in these that had autobiographical undertones.

Wodehouse was an intensely private person who disliked talking about himself and regarded his inner feelings as sacrosanct; to publicise them would make him feel, like one of his characters, 'as if he was being divested of most of his more important garments in a crowded thoroughfare'. He was a kind and gentle man who found it difficult to dislike anyone, but he did have an aversion to anyone who tried to break down the barrier of privacy with which he surrounded himself and probe too deeply into the image of himself he had created for public consumption. The famous author and broadcaster, Malcolm Muggeridge, who knew him well and interviewed him for a BBC programme, wrote of him: 'As with all imaginative people there is an area of inner reserve in Wodehouse which one never penetrates.'

Left to himself he would have fended off all intruders and had nothing to do with them, but for one of his fame and (for part of his life) notoriety the pressure was too great, and when his strong-minded wife, Ethel, decided that he must relent, he had to submit himself to a number of interviews and interrogations. He even produced three volumes of autobiography. But these did not tell the whole story. In them he wrote of his life in general terms and gave his views on a variety of subjects, but seldom profoundly and never on anything intimate. Before embarking on them he made it clear that the main purpose of them was entertainment; truth was secondary. The basis of one of the books was the letters he had written to his great friend, William Townend, but from the outset he was candid that he felt free to alter these as much as he liked:

The great thing, as I see it, is not to feel ourselves confined to the actual letters. I mean, nobody knows what was actually in the letters, so we can fake as much as we like ... I have always wanted to write my autobiography but felt too self-conscious. This will be a way of doing the thing obliquely.

But if Wodehouse revealed little of himself in his 'oblique' autobiography, he might have done more in his novels. He could put much of himself into his fictional characters and make them say things which he himself felt but which he shied away from uttering on his own account. For example, in the autobiographies there is no mention of his feelings on becoming engaged to Ethel; but is there not a strong likelihood that they were similar, if not identical, to those of Ashe Marson towards Joan Valentine in *Something Fresh*? And can there be much doubt that his description of Lord Emsworth in the same book is a self-portrait?

Other people worried about all sorts of things — strikes, wars, suffragettes, diminishing birth rates, the growing materialism of the age and a score of similar subjects. Lord Emsworth never worried. Nature had equipped him with a mind so admirably constructed for withstanding the disagreeableness of life that, if an unpleasant thought entered it, it passed out again a moment later.

It has been the object of the author, then, to seek out passages in the works of fiction with autobiographical implications, and fit them into the Wodehouse story. It has also been his intent to create a portrait of an unusual genius full of contradictions: one from whom, seated in front of a typewriter, there came a profusion of words that brought laughter to millions, but who in company became tongue-tied and ill at ease and seldom laughed or made a joke; one who was so dominated by his art that wherever he might be – luxury hotel, ship's cabin, railway carriage, internment camp, police station, even a maternity ward – he could so isolate himself from his surroundings as to become absorbed in his writing; one who was acknowledged by the greatest writers of his time as 'the master' and 'the head of our profession', but whose own reading tastes were for detective stories and what he himself called 'trash' rather than for the great classics; and one who, strictly as he might guard his privacy, nevertheless found himself at times in the glare of the arc lights.

Chapter 1

Aunt calling to aunt like mastodons bellowing across primeval swamps.

The ring of a ball on a cricket bat, the green of the pitch, the white of the flannels and the sound of schoolboy cheers.

An abnormal proficiency at games has apparently destroyed all desire to realise the more serious issues of life (school report).

Few authors have given so much pleasure and caused so much laughter as P. G. Wodehouse. He has been read worldwide and some of his characters, such as Jeeves, Bertie Wooster, Lord Emsworth and Gussie Fink-Nottle, have become household names. On his ninetieth birthday he was hailed by a group of leading writers of the time as 'an inimitable international institution and master humorist'.

Pelham Grenville Wodehouse was born in Guildford in 1881. At the time his mother was on leave from Hong Kong where his father, Ernest Wodehouse, was in the Colonial Service. Ernest came from a family with aristocratic connections, including in his ancestry Mary Boleyn, sister of Anne Boleyn. Pelham's mother, Eleanor Wodehouse, was one of thirteen children of a well-to-do

London clergyman; she was also a cousin of Cardinal John Henry Newman, a religious leader and one of the great writers of the nineteenth century.

Although he later denied it, there can be little doubt that Pelham, or Plum as he came to be called, had a bleak and loveless childhood. At the age of two he was sent from Hong Kong to England with his two elder brothers, who were going to school there, and put into the care of a series of ladies who, though not necessarily related, were always known as aunts. Little is known of these aunts, but it seems that they were respectable ladies, kindly in their way but strict and ready 'to be cruel to be kind'. No doubt, like other children of that time, Plum was brought up to be always on his best behaviour, to speak only when spoken to and generally to be seen and not heard. In later life Plum hardly ever mentioned his childhood, but seems to have borne no resentment about it. In his light-hearted autobiography, *Over Seventy*, he dismissed it cursorily in one sentence: 'My childhood went like a breeze from start to finish with everyone I met understanding me perfectly.' But then throughout his life Plum was the most uncomplaining of men; he never felt bitterness or self-pity even when life was at its hardest. Somehow he always adapted and found contentment. And it seems that in childhood, as later in life, he was able to escape from adversity in his writing. For as long as he could remember he was enthralled by the idea of making up stories. One of these, written at the age of seven, has been preserved and it is remarkable for a child of that age:

About five years ago in a wood there was a Thrush, who built her Nest in a Poplar tree, and sang so beautifully that all the worms came up from their holes and ants laid down their burdens and the crickets stopped their mirth, and moths settled all in a row to hear her. She sang a song as if she were in Heaven – going higher and higher as she sang. At last the song was done and the bird came down panting. Thank you said all the creatures.

Now my story is ended.
Pelham G. Wodehouse.

But although Plum had no hard feelings about his upbringing, he certainly looked back on it without pleasure. In his books he never wrote about childhood and, indeed, showed a marked distaste for it. Whenever children appear it is almost always in an unflattering light. Young girls are sometimes allowed a measure of charm, but young boys never. These are invariably creatures of horror – stout, sulky, greedy and urgently in need of 'a swift slosh on the base of the skull with a black-jack'. 'Boyhood,' he wrote, 'like measles is one of those complaints which a man should catch young and have done with.'

If Plum never cared to think about his childhood and dismissed it as of no importance, he was, nevertheless, permanently marked by it. For all his life he was at heart a Victorian with Victorian values and a distrust of modern ideas. He was to go on writing well into the age of the so-called 'permissive society', but he never availed himself of the licence employed with such relish by other writers. To the end his books retained a certain propriety both as regards language and the way his characters behaved.

Another permanent effect of his childhood on Plum might also be noted – a strong aversion to, amounting almost to a fixation on 'women of rather markedly overwhelming personality', particularly aunts. His books are full of them and they are always ogres – 'she-dragons', 'human vampire bats' – who make life difficult and disagreeable for everyone around them, most notably like Bertie Wooster's Aunt Agatha:

> *When I was a kid at school she was always able to turn me inside out with a single glance. There's about five-foot-nine of Aunt Agatha, topped off with a beaky nose, an eagle eye and a lot of grey hair, and the general effect is pretty formidable ... My experience is that when Aunt Agatha wants you to do a thing you do it, or else you find yourself wondering why those fellows in the olden days made such a fuss when they had trouble with the Spanish Inquisition.*

And Aunt Julia was almost as bad:

> *My Aunt Julia lacks Aunt Agatha's punch, but in a quiet way she has always made me feel, from boyhood up, that I was a poor worm. The difference between the two is that Aunt Agatha conveys the impression that she considers me personally responsible for all the sin and sorrow in the world, while Aunt Julia's manner seems to suggest that I am more to be pitied than censured.*

Plum must surely have suffered more from his 'aunts' than he ever let on.

Although Plum remained forever a Victorian, there

was one matter in which he deviated: he had no religious beliefs, and this may have been due in part to the rigour of the religious practices imposed on him in childhood. Certainly these were extensive – family prayers each morning, frequent churchgoing and strict observance of the Sabbath. For his tribulations on these occasions, Plum was later to exact a measure of revenge in his books where the Church, and more particularly clergymen, came in for some gentle mockery. Church occasions, such as mothers' outings, school treats and concerts in aid of the church organ fund, were always hilarious and chaotic. And the clergy were invariably figures of fun: a pale young curate who had been bullied at theological college; a muscular vicar who nearly came to blows with his bishop about the number of orphreys on his chasubles, and with his curate about whether at Harvest Festival a pumpkin should be placed in the apse or the clerestory; and a bishop (also muscular, having been twice winner of the Curates Open Heavyweight Championship) who ran amok after taking an overdose of Buck-U-Uppo. And all Wodehouse clerics talk in exaggerated vicar speak. Thus the Bishop of Stortford in reply to an enquiry about his lumbago:

I find the pain sensibly diminished, thank you, Mulliner – in fact, almost non-existent. The pleasant weather seems to do me good. For lo! The winter is past, the rain is over and gone; the flowers appear on the earth; the time of the singing birds is come, and the voice of the turtle is heard in the land. Song of Solomon 2:11–12.

Vicar and curate at loggerheads

A marked distaste for old-fashioned Sundays is also to be found in Plum's books. It is likely he was speaking for himself when, in *Bill the Conqueror*, an elderly gentleman finds himself on a Sunday in a nightclub, and looks back on the Sundays of his youth:

Nothing in this modern life of ours is more significant than the attitude of the good and respectable towards Sunday evening. Places like this are the outward and visible signs of the inward and spiritual change that has taken place in the life of the English family. Twenty years ago a man of my decent stodginess and unblemished reputation would never have dreamed of moving out of his home on Sunday night. Twenty years ago I would have spent the concluding hours of the Sabbath surrounded by my loved ones beneath our own roof-tree. There would have been supper, consisting of rather red cold beef, rather wet salad, cold clammy apple pie, blancmange, and a very big very yellow cheese. This would have been followed by hymns in the drawing room – or possibly, if our views were a little lax, by some round game played with pencils and pieces of paper. The fact that I am here and strongly tempted to drop a sardine on the head of the bald gentleman down below is due to what they call the March of Progress.

Plum seems to have had an aversion to Sunday suppers. Reference is also made to them in *Psmith in the City*:

. . . probably the most depressing meal in existence. There is a chill discomfort in the round of beef, an icy severity about the open jam tart. The blancmange shivers miserably.

9

Sunday supper

In treating religion as a subject for comedy Plum did so without disrespect, let alone profanity. Although an unbeliever, he yet had great affection for the Church and considerable knowledge of its ways. In *The Inimitable Jeeves* he recalls nostalgically evensong in a village church:

There's something about evening service in a country church that makes a fellow feel drowsy and peaceful. Sort of end-of-a-perfect day feeling . . . They had left the door open, and the air was full of a mixed scent of trees and honeysuckle and mildew and villagers' Sunday clothes . . . The last rays of the setting sun shone through the stained-glass windows, birds were twittering in the trees, the women's

*dresses crackled gently in the stillness. Peaceful. That's what
I am driving at. I felt peaceful.*

At the age of thirteen Plum was sent to Dulwich
College, a public school in south-east London. There had
been an idea that he should go into the Navy, but he
was saved from this by weak eyesight, surely a merciful
reprieve. One cannot imagine Plum on the quarterdeck.
His family had no particular connections with Dulwich,
but his father had been greatly attracted by the district,
still largely open country, while passing through it on the
train. For Plum it could not have been a more fortunate
choice; his six years there were to be, as he later described
them, 'unbroken bliss'.

At that time it was not unusual for boys to become
devoted to their public schools in a way unknown today;
but Plum's love for Dulwich was something special. This
was not, perhaps, surprising. Up until then his life had
been spent in households where there was much
solemnity but not much warmth or laughter. At Dulwich
he was to find for the first time excitement and
comradeship – the delights of being part of a community,
living in close association with others and sharing their
lives. It must surely have been partly autobiographical
when, in *Mike*, he wrote of a schoolboy at Sedleigh
School:

*To Adair Sedleigh was almost a religion. Both his parents
were dead; his guardian, with whom he spent the holidays,
was a man with neuralgia at one end of him and gout at
the other; and the only really pleasant times Adair had had,*

as far back as he could remember, he owed to Sedleigh. The place had grown on him, absorbed him.

As a scholar Plum gained no great distinction at Dulwich; he was above average but no more. And although he was one of the editors of the school magazine, he was not noted for any great literary talent. One who later in life was to be described as 'a lord of language', had to be content at school with an English essay report of 'not very strong'.

Certainly it was not the academic life at Dulwich which attracted Plum. What endeared the place to him for ever, and made him a considerable figure while he was there, was his prowess at games. He was in the cricket eleven for two years and the rugby fifteen for one. And here he found a fervour and excitement he was never to know again. In the course of a highly successful career he must have had many thrilling moments but nothing to compare with those experiences on the playing fields of Dulwich. In *Money for Nothing* he described these vividly:

Only once in his life before could he remember having felt as he felt now, and that was one raw November evening at school at the close of the football match against Marlborough when, after battling wearily through a long half hour to preserve the slenderest of all possible leads, he had heard the referee's whistle sound through the rising mists and had stood up, bruised and battered and covered with mud, to the realisation that the game was over and won.

Plum's love of cricket and rugby and, to a lesser extent, boxing was something he never lost. For the rest of his life the results of Dulwich matches were always to him the most important item of news in a newspaper. Watching Dulwich matches was his favourite occupation, and school rugby and cricket his favourite topics of conversation. On one occasion, when he went to watch a Dulwich match, the excitement was too much for him and he had to go away until the match was over and the result could be broken to him.

Plum was the eternal schoolboy, caught in a time capsule. For the rest of his life his disposition, outlook and spoken word were essentially those of a seventeen-year-old schoolboy.

Chapter 2

I proved to be the most inefficient clerk whose trouser seat ever polished the surface of a high stool.

If there was a moment in the course of my banking career when I had the foggiest notion of what it was all about, I am unable to recall it.

While Plum was at Dulwich his father had to take early retirement from the Colonial Service because of sunstroke, said to have been brought on by an unwise bet that he could walk round the perimeter of Hong Kong island in a given time. On the return of his parents to England Plum, for the first time in his life, had the opportunity to get to know them, but this he did not find easy. His father was affable and kindly, but also somewhat remote. His mother Plum found aloof and forbidding – 'more of an aunt than a mother' he later wrote. Harsh words indeed from him.

Soon after arriving in England Ernest and Eleanor Wodehouse took a house in the small Shropshire village of Stableford, and it was here, during the school holidays, that Plum first became acquainted with the English countryside. It made a deep and indelible impression on

14

him. Even though he lived in it for only a tiny part of his life, most of his best known stories were to be set in the heart of rural England, usually Shropshire, where he located Blandings Castle, surely one of the most famous stately homes in fiction.

English villages seem to have occupied a special place in Plum's heart, and in his books he delighted in depicting their quaint customs, sleepy atmosphere and eccentric personalities. He has given no description of Stableford, but perhaps Rudge-in-the-Vale, a Shropshire village in *Money for Nothing*, is not unlike it:

> *The picturesque village of Rudge-in-the-Vale dozed in the summer sunshine. Along its narrow High Street the only signs of life visible were a cat stropping its backbone against the Jubilee Watering Trough, some flies doing deep-breathing exercises on the hot window-sills, and a little group of serious thinkers who, propped up against the wall of the Carmody Arms, were waiting for that establishment to open. At no time is there ever much doing in Rudge's main thoroughfare, but the hour at which a stranger, entering it, is least likely to suffer the illusion that he has strayed into Broadway, Piccadilly or the Rue de Rivoli is at two o'clock on a warm afternoon in July.*
>
> *You will find Rudge-in-the-Vale, if you search carefully, in that pleasant section of rural England where the grey stone of Gloucestershire gives place to Worcestershire's old red brick. Quiet – in fact, almost unconscious, it nestles beside the tiny river Skirme and lets the world go by, somnolently content with its Norman church, its eleven public houses, its Pop, – to quote the Automobile Guide – of*

3,541, and its only effort in the direction of modern progress, the emporium of Chas. Bywater, Chemist.

Maybe too Stableford had a Village Hall, and this could have been like the one of King's Peverill, described in *The Mating Season*:

The Village Hall stood in the middle of the High Street, just abaft the duck-pond. Erected in the year 1881 by Sir Quintin Deverill, Bart, a man who didn't know much about architecture but knew what he liked, it was one of those mid-Victorian jobs in glazed red brick which always seem to bob up in these old-world hamlets and do so much to encourage the drift to the towns. Its interior, like those of all the joints of its kind I've ever come across, was dingy and fuggy and smelled in about equal proportions of apples, chalk, damp plaster, Boy Scouts and the sturdy English peasantry.

And perhaps too Stableford held an annual village fete, similar to the one at Ashendon Oakshott in *Uncle Dynamite*:

A word about this fete. It was the high spot of Ashendon Oakshott's social year, when all that was bravest and fairest in the village assembled in the Manor grounds and made various kinds of whoopee. Races were run, country dances danced, bonny babies judged in order of merit in the big tent, and teas and buns consumed in almost incredible quantities. Picture a blend of the Derby and a garden party at Buckingham Palace, add Belshazzar's Feast, and you have the Ashendon Oakshott Fete.

But much as he loved rural England, it seems that Plum was not altogether at ease living in the midst of it. If he had been left alone in a small room to get on with his writing, he would have been content; but some social life was required of him and this he found very trying:

The only thing I didn't like in my formative or Stableford period was the social stuff. Owners of big estates round about would keep inviting me for the weekend . . . Even today I'm about as pronounced an oaf who ever went around with his lower jaw dropping and a glassy look in his eye, but you have literally no conception what I was like in my early twenties . . . Picture to yourself a Trappist monk with large feet and a tendency to upset tables with priceless china on them, and you will have the young Wodehouse.

Large, clumsy, muscular young men were to appear often in the Wodehouse works, and Plum always treated them kindly.

In his retirement Ernest Wodehouse had a reasonably adequate pension, but it was paid in rupees, the value of which fluctuated considerably, and there were times when the Wodehouse finances became stretched:

The wolf was not actually whining at the door and there was always a little something in the kitty for the butcher and the grocer, but the finances would not run to anything in the nature of a splash.

Economies became necessary, and one of these was that Plum would not be able to go to a university. This was a great disappointment to him, as he would dearly have loved to get a cricket or rugby blue. The painful interview with his father when the news was broken to him was surely re-enacted closely in *Psmith in the City* when the sporting hero, Mike Jackson, suffered the same fate.

> *Mike looked at him blankly. This could only mean one thing. He was not to go to the Varsity. But why? What had happened? . . .*
>
> *'Aren't I going up to Cambridge, father?' stammered Mike.*
>
> *'I'm afraid not, Mike . . . I won't go into details . . . but I've lost a very large sum of money since I saw you last. So large that we shall have to economise in every way . . . I'm afraid you will have to start earning your living. I know it's a terrible disappointment to you, old chap.'*
>
> *'Oh, that's all right,' said Mike thickly. There seemed to be something in his throat, preventing him from speaking. 'If there was any possible way——'*
>
> *'No, it's all right, father, really. I don't mind a bit. It's awfully rough luck on you losing all that.'*

It might not have been quite such a blow had he been allowed to do what he really wanted which was to live quietly and inexpensively at home and make a career for himself as a writer. But this his father would not allow. Ernest Wodehouse was a conscientious parent and conceived it his duty to educate his sons and then launch them into safe, reliable jobs; and freelance writing did not, he considered, fall into this category.

And so, after leaving Dulwich, Plum was obliged to

take employment in the offices of the Hong Kong and
Shanghai Bank, where he was to spend two years. They
were probably the unhappiest of his life. He may not
have been quite such an inept bank clerk as he later made
out, but he was all too clearly a square peg in a round
hole and must have suffered hours of boredom and
frustration. However, it was not in his nature to be self-
pitying and later he described his experiences in the Bank
with great good humour in *Psmith in the City*. This tells
how Mike, a public schoolboy not unlike Plum – shy,
stolid, country-loving and a notable cricketer – was
compelled to work in a bank instead of going to a
university. His sufferings there were surely based on Plum's
own. In the first place there was the gruesome experience
of finding a cheap lodging:

> *In answer to Mike's knock a female person opened the
> door. In appearance she resembled a pantomime dame . . .
> Her most recent occupation seemed to have been something
> with a good deal of yellow soap in it . . . She wiped a pair
> of steaming hands on her apron and regarded Mike with
> an eye which would have been markedly expressionless in a
> boiled fish.*
>
> *'Was there anything?' she asked.*

And then the horror of the room he felt obliged to rent:

> *It was a repulsive room. One of those characterless rooms
> which are only found in furnished apartments. To Mike,
> used to the comforts of his bedroom at home and the cheerful
> simplicity of a school dormitory, it seemed about the most*

dismal spot he had ever struck. A sort of Sargasso Sea among bedrooms.

To the end of his life Plum retained a horror of rented rooms. Whenever they occurred in his books they were always depicted as seedy, depressing places full of antimacassars, china dogs, wax flowers and, as often as not, the Infant Samuel at prayer. The part of London in which Plum took his first lodging was Chelsea, perhaps because he imagined it to be full of struggling artists and writers, one of whom he hoped one day to be himself. Chelsea was not then the fashionable and expensive part of London it has since become; much of it was cheap and down at heel, like Budge Street portrayed in *Uncle Dynamite*:

Budge Street, Chelsea, in the heart of London's artistic quarter, is, like so many streets in the hearts of artistic quarters, dark, dirty, dingy and depressing. Its residents would appear to be great readers and very fond of fruit, for tattered newspapers can always be found fluttering about its sidewalks and old banana skins, cores of apples, plum stones and squashed strawberries lying in large quantities in its gutters. Its cats are stringy, hard-boiled cats, who look as if they were contemplating, or had just finished perpetrating, a series of murders of the more brutal type.

Having found himself a lodging, Plum then proceeded to his first day's work at the Hong Kong and Shanghai Bank, and this could have been similar to Mike's at the New Asiatic Bank:

He followed the human stream till he reached the Mansion House, and eventually found himself at the massive building of the New Asiatic Bank. Inside the bank seemed to be in a state of confusion. Men were moving about in an apparently irresolute manner. Nobody seemed actually to be working. As a matter of fact, the business of a bank does not start very early in the morning. Mike had arrived before things had really begun to move . . . After a while things began to settle down. The stir and confusion gradually ceased. All down the length of the bank figures could be seen, seated on stools and writing hieroglyphics in large ledgers.

At first Mike was put to work in the postage department, entering and stamping letters (the only work in the bank, Plum confessed later, he felt able to do). He found himself under:

. . . a fussy little brute who used to buzz out of his den with the esprit and animation of a clockwork toy . . . a kind of human sodawater bottle who fizzed over with questions, reproofs and warnings.

In time came the lunch hour, for City workers the most important event of the day:

It is the keynote of their day. It is an oasis in a desert of ink and ledgers. Conversation in a City office deals in the morning with what one is going to have for lunch, and in the afternoon with what one has had for lunch.

21

Then at last the day's work came to an end:

Mike felt as if he had been sitting at his desk for weeks when the hour for departure came. A bank's day ends gradually, reluctantly as it were. At about five there is a sort of stir, not unlike the stir in a theatre when the curtain is on the point of falling. Ledgers are closed with a bang. Men stand about and talk for a moment or two before going to the basement for their hats and coats. Then, at irregular intervals, forms pass down the central aisle and out through the swing doors . . . Gradually the electric lights go out . . . The procession becomes more regular; and eventually the place is left to darkness and the night watchman.

Chapter 3

Worse bilge than mine may have been submitted to the editors of London in 1901 and 1902, but I should think it very unlikely.

If only a writer keeps on writing, something generally breaks eventually.

I sit down at my typewriter and curse a bit.

Plum was never in any doubt that a banking career was not for him. He was determined to leave the Hong Kong and Shanghai Bank at the earliest possible opportunity. If he did not, there was a danger that he might be sent to the Far East as a bank manager. To some this might seem an exciting and glamorous prospect. In *Psmith in the City* Mike's loquacious friend, Psmith, had a rosy vision of life there:

'I seem to see you in armchair, fanned by devoted coolies, telling some Eastern potentate that you can give him five minutes. I understand that being in a bank in the Far East is one of the world's softest jobs. Millions of natives hang on your lightest word. Enthusiastic rajahs draw you aside and press jewels into your hand as a token of respect and

esteem. When on an elephant's back you pass, somebody beats on a booming brass gong! The Banker of Bhong!'

To Plum, however, the idea was appalling:

The picture of myself managing a branch was one I preferred not to examine too closely. I couldn't have managed a whelkstall.

And so every spare moment he had, while he was at the bank, Plum spent writing; writing anything – short stories, comic verse, serials and articles on almost any subject.

Most of Plum's first efforts were never published. 'I had a collection of rejection slips,' he wrote, 'with which I could have papered a good sized banqueting hall.' But some of them did find their way into print – while he was at the bank about eighty – and although he was only paid a pound or two for them, sometimes less, it was a start. He was beginning to establish himself in a keenly competitive profession. The big question was when he should take the plunge and leave the bank. The matter came to a head when he was offered a job at three guineas a week (at that time just a living wage) on the *Globe* magazine. It was only for five weeks while someone was away on holiday, but to Plum it was an opportunity not to be missed. Later in his books he was fond of quoting the famous lines from *Julius Caesar*:

There is a tide in the affairs of men,
Which, taken at the flood, leads on to fortune;
Omitted, all the voyage of their life
Is bound in shallows and in miseries.

Perhaps these lines occurred to him then, for he made up his mind that the moment had arrived. And so he bade a none too fond farewell to the Hong Kong and Shanghai Bank, and embarked on a full-time career as a writer.

The *Globe* was a good starting point for Plum. His particular task was to fill a column called 'By the Way'. This involved reading through the morning papers, picking out items of news and then writing something funny about them. This might be a story, a witty remark or comic verse; but every day the column had to be filled – and in a matter of hours. This proved a valuable experience; at the end of five weeks Plum had discovered what being a professional writer involved. In *Not George Washington*, a semi-autobiographical story, he wrote:

> *I had learned the art of writing against time. I had learned to ignore noise, which, for a writer in London, is the most valuable quality of all. Every day I had to turn out my stuff with the hum of the Strand traffic in my ears, varied by occasional barrel-organs, the whistling of popular songs by the printers, whose window faced ours, and the clatter of the typewriter in the next room. Often I had to turn out a paragraph or a verse while listening and making appropriate replies to some other member of the staff who had wandered into our room to pass the time of day or read out a bit of his own stuff which had happened to please him particularly. All this gave me a power of concentration without which writing is difficult in this city of noises.*

Even before his stint at the *Globe* came to an end Plum realised that, if he was going to survive as a writer, his output of the printed word would have to be greatly increased. What he would like to have done was to write a full-length novel (he had written *The Pothunters* while at the bank), but this would have taken time, and he needed money at once. So, for the time being, he had to turn out bits and pieces. These were for all sorts of publications — *Fun, Tit-Bits, Scraps, Answers, Sandow's Physical Culture Magazine* among others. Nor could he afford the luxury of writing only what he liked. It was necessary for him to produce what the editors of magazines wanted. And if this meant writing trash full of sensation and 'mushy sentiment', he would do it.

Fortunately Plum did not have to write trash for long; for he soon discovered a type of story which he could write well and for which there was at that time a great demand. For some reason school stories were especially popular in Edwardian England. Classics such as *Tom Brown's Schooldays* and *Stalky and Co.* were on every shelf, but, in addition, school stories appeared every week in boys' magazines. Of these the best known were *Gem* and *Magnet*, which told of the exploits of Billy Bunter and others at Greyfriars School. Today it is likely that most readers would find these stories heavy going, even distasteful. Slow-moving and long-winded, blatantly snobbish, with no violence or romance, let alone sex, they were supposed to be about life in English Public Schools. However, at that time they were read avidly by all classes of reader, especially by those who had not been to Public Schools; and it is believed that they had considerable influence on people's attitudes and ideas. With Plum, after his idyllic years at Dulwich, they had always been great favourites, and he loved writing them. At first he wrote them in serial form for *The Captain* and *Public School Magazine*, and these proved so popular that they were then published in volume form.

In many ways Plum's school stories were like others of the time, full of dormitory rags, study teas, 'ripping good sorts', and 'dirty rotters'. The great heroes were always the games bloods rather than the scholars, although the latter were tolerated provided they did not work too hard and did not show off their erudition, in which case they became 'swots' and figures of fun. Invariably the high spot of a school story was a thrilling finish to a games match, epitomised in Sir Henry Newbolt's famous lines from *Vitai Lampada*:

> *There's a breathless hush in the close tonight –*
> *Ten to make and the match to win –*
> *A bumping pitch and a blinding light,*
> *An hour to play and the last man in.*

But Plum's school stories were not entirely similar to the others of that time. In the first place they contained nothing really disagreeable. At his schools there was no serious bullying; no bloodcurdling fights; boys were not flogged or roasted. Also in Plum's stories there was no high moral tone. Unlike Rudyard Kipling and Dean Farrar, Plum had no interest in putting across a message or in exhorting his readers to become good Christian men and women. He was concerned only to entertain. Of course the boys in his stories had to abide by the rules, customs and traditions of their school. They must wash, respect their elders, never funk anything and never 'show side' (boast). Otherwise, apart from always playing games as hard as they could, nothing much else was expected of them.

Although they had great success at the time, few people today would regard Plum's school stories as being among his greatest works. They are quite different from the later stories about Bertie Wooster and Lord Emsworth. The style is less flippant, in places even serious; they are comedies rather than farces. However, they were probably the books Plum most enjoyed writing. In old age he told a friend that his favourite book was *Mike* because it brought back to him 'the ring of a ball on a cricket bat, the green of the pitch, the white of the flannels and the sound of schoolboy cheers'. Plum's heart was always at Dulwich; the rest of life was an anticlimax.

By 1904, two years after he had left the bank, Plum could look back on his achievements with some satisfaction. His school stories were being published regularly and he had been given a permanent job on the *Globe* at an increased salary. In addition he had made a start in a field which was to be of increasing importance in his life, writing for the theatre. Plum was never a successful playwright. Although a supreme craftsman as a novelist, he never mastered the technique of writing plays. But he had considerable talent for composing light verse, and with the coming into fashion of musical comedies, there was scope for him in writing the words of the songs. Here he had instant success, and was taken on by Sir Seymour Hicks, a well known actor-manager, as permanent lyricist in his company.

Plum's career, then, was advancing rapidly, but this meant very hard work and long hours. He seldom went out in the evenings and his social life was almost non-existent. One memorable visit he did make was to a great hero of his, W. S. Gilbert, the writer of the Savoy Operas. This meeting between two of the great humorists of the English language might have been a famous event, but it proved to be something of a disaster. At the dinner table Gilbert embarked on a long story and was building up to a tremendous climax when Plum laughed loudly at the wrong moment and spoiled it completely. He recalled later that Gilbert gave him a look of such hatred that 'it seared my very soul'.

An event of major importance in Plum's life at that time was his first visit to America. In those days the sea voyage cost only £10 and took nine days; and as he had five weeks holiday due to him from the *Globe*, he decided to go. The visit made a deep impression on him. There was something about the American way of life that appealed to him greatly. In time America was to change his life and become his home, but the only consequence of his first visit was that he found a new and lucrative market for his works.

By 1906, when he was twenty-five, Plum could be said to have established himself as a writer. By then he was earning over £500 a year, on which he could live quite comfortably. He had even managed to save a fair-sized sum for future emergencies; but then came an unfortunate accident. He was persuaded to spend £450 on buying a motor car, which he then proceeded to drive without learning how to do so. The result was that he drove straight into a hedge. Plum was not mechanically minded and had no idea how to get the car out of the hedge, and so, as there was no one around to help him, he simply left the car where it was, caught a train back to London and did nothing more about it.

Chapter 4

Ukridge

'She had wanted to borrow my aunt's brooch,' said Ukridge, 'but I was firm and wouldn't let her have it – partly on principle and partly because I had pawned it the day before.'

'I didn't know, Corky, if you had ever done the fine, dignified thing, refusing to accept money because it was tainted and there wasn't enough of it,' said Ukridge.

'Fibs or, shall we say, the artistic mouldings of the unshapely clay of truth'

Although the mishap of the motor car had been a serious blow to Plum's finances, amends were soon to be made by the success of his first adult novel, *Love Among the Chickens* (1906). These were not school stories but concerned the adventures and misfortunes of one of Plum's best known characters, Stanley Featherstonehaugh Ukridge (pronounced Yewkridge). Ukridge was based in part on a friend of Plum's called Herbert Westbrook, who had at times caused him much trouble and vexation – endlessly borrowing money, helping himself to clothes without asking, and even, on one occasion, pawning his banjo.

It is unlikely that Westbrook was quite such an outrageous character as Ukridge. Exuberant, chaotic, utterly irresponsible, addressing everyone he met as 'laddie' or 'old horse', Ukridge plunged from one disaster to another. He had been expelled from school for breaking out and attending a local fete, disguised in scarlet whiskers and a false nose, but unaware that he was wearing the school cap. From then on he had had one wild scheme after another for making huge and instant fortunes; these included chicken farming, dog training, bookmaking and promoting a heavyweight boxer. For a time he lived with a prim, respectable aunt in Wimbledon, but this came to an end when it emerged that, while she was away, he had been using her house as an illegal gambling joint and her garden for National Buttercup Day in aid of a charity which was, of course, himself. When he left he took with him her six Pekingese dogs in order to start up his dogs' training college; but, of course, this scheme, like all others, came to grief. Large bills were run up with local tradesmen who, understandably, expected to be repaid. This caused Ukridge furious indignation:

'It's a little hard. Upon my Sam it's a little hard. I come down here to inaugurate a vast business and do the natives a bit of good by establishing a growing industry in their midst, and the first thing you know they turn round and bite the hand that was going to feed them. I've been hampered and rattled by these bloodsuckers ever since I got here. A little trust, a little sympathy, a little of the good

old give-and-take spirit – that was all I asked. And what
happened? They wanted a bit on account.'

Another of Ukridge's harebrained and fraudulent
schemes was the Accident Syndicate. This too needed
capital both from Ukridge and his associates. His methods
of raising it were typical, and Plum must have related
them with considerable feelings:

'Gentlemen,' said Ukridge, 'it would seem that the company
requires more capital. How about it, old horses? Let's get
together in a frank business-like cards-on-the-table spirit, and
see what can be done. I can raise ten bob.'

'What!' cried the entire assembled company, amazed.
'How?'

'I'll pawn a banjo.'

'You haven't got a banjo.'

'No, but George Tupper has, and I know where he
keeps it.'

The Accident Syndicate required that one of its
members (chosen by lot) should have an accident. But
in the event the victim proved reluctant to go through
with the idea. Once again Ukridge was full of indignation:

'Any bloke with a sense of loyalty and an appreciation
of what it means to the rest of us would have rushed out
and found some means of fulfilling his duty long ago. You
don't even grasp at the opportunities that come your way.
Only yesterday I saw you draw back when a single step into
the road would have had a truck bumping into you.'

'Well, it's not so easy to let a truck bump into you,' [said Teddy Weeks]

'Nonsense. It only requires a little ordinary resolution. Use your imagination, man. Try to think that a child has fallen down in the street – a little golden-haired child,' said Ukridge deeply affected. 'And a dashed great cab or something comes rolling up. The kid's mother is standing on the pavement, helpless, her hands clasped in agony. "Dammit," she cries, "will no one save my darling?" "Yes, by George," you shout, "I will". And out you jump and the thing's over in half a second. I don't know what you're making such a fuss about.'

'Yes, but—' said Teddy Weeks.

'I'm told, what's more, it isn't a bit painful. A sort of dull shock, that's all.'

'Who told you that?'

'I forget. Someone.'

Ukridge is not one of the more likeable of Plum's characters; he is too much of a sponger, too gross, too much of a menace to his friends and, indeed, to society at large. He is, in almost every way, the complete opposite of Plum himself. Plum was shy and quiet and kept himself to himself; Ukridge was noisy and brash and overflowed in all directions. Perhaps it was because he was so different that Plum was so fond of him and went on writing stories about him into his old age. Ukridge had some amiable qualities, but it might be said of him, as Plum said of another of his characters: 'Those who loved him best were those who saw least of him.'

Psmith

My reports from Eton were simply scurrilous. There's a libel action in every sentence.

Are you the chap with the eyeglass who jaws all the time?

A more remarkable and more attractive character to appear in the Wodehouse works at this time was Psmith. His real name was plain Smith, but he decided 'there were so many Smiths in the world that a little variety might well be introduced'. So he added a 'p' which, it was important to remember, was silent 'as in phthisis, psychic and ptarmigan'. Psmith's first appearance came in *Mike*, the last of the Wodehouse school stories, which was different from previous ones. These had been semi-serious, even earnest at times; but *Mike* was entirely frivolous. School life became something of a romp, and everything, even cricket, was treated light-heartedly. And at centre stage, leading the revels was Psmith. Certainly he was an unusual schoolboy:

A very long, thin youth, with a solemn face and immaculate clothes, was leaning against the mantelpiece. As Mike entered, he fumbled in his top left waistcoat pocket, produced an eyeglass attached to a cord, and fixed it in his right eye. With the help of this aid to vision he inspected Mike in silence for a while, then having flicked an invisible speck of dust from the left sleeve of his coat, he spoke.

Psmith was said to have been based on Rupert D'Oyly Carte, son of the founder of the Gilbert and Sullivan opera company, who had caused quite a stir at Winchester College by his behaviour and general demeanour. Like him Psmith was tall, elegant and gracious and regarded his fellow men benevolently, although with more than a touch of condescension, usually through a well-polished monocle. And whatever difficulties surrounded him, he was never at a loss for a word, usually a spate of words, which left his audience dazed and sometimes tottering. In spite of his aristocratic background Psmith affected a form of socialism, and addressed everyone as 'comrade'. He did not, however, allow his political creed to interfere with his way of life, which was as expensive as possible. His definition of socialism (psocialism, as one writer dubbed it) was unorthodox: 'You work for equal distribution of property, and start by collaring all you can and sitting on it.'

In *Mike* Psmith is to be found at Sedleigh School with his friend, Mike Jackson. He has been sent there because at Eton he had been totally idle, but he was no more industrious at Sedleigh. Here one of his first acts was to join the Archaeological Society run by his bumbling housemaster, Mr Outwood; but not, as he told Mike, out of any great interest in archaeology:

> *You and I, hand in hand, will search the countryside for ruined abbeys. We will snare the elusive fossil together. Above all we will go out of bounds. We shall thus improve our minds, and have a jolly good time as well . . . From what*

I saw of Comrade Outwood during our brief interview, I shouldn't think he is one of the lynx-eyed contingent. With tact we ought to be able to slip away from the merry throng of fossil chasers, and do a bit on our own account . . .

Having inspired confidence by the docility of our demeanour, let us slip away, and brood apart for a while. Roman camps, to be absolutely accurate, give me the pip. And I never want to see another putrid fossil in my life. Let us find some shady nook where a man may lie on his back for a while.'

Another reason for joining the Archaeological Society was that he would avoid cricket. In fact Psmith was not a bad cricketer, but did not want to play partly because, if he could not play for Eton, he did not want to play for any other school team, and partly because the last time he had played had been in a village match where he had been subjected to an awesome ordeal:

'I was caught at point by a man in braces, and it would have been madness to risk another such shock to my system. My nerves are so exquisitely balanced that a thing of that sort takes years off my life.'

Psmith is next to be found in Plum's partly autobiographical novel, *Psmith in the City*, where he joins Mike Jackson in the offices of the New Asiatic Bank. Here too he is a disruptive influence. The objectionable manager, Mr Bickersteth, he persecutes on every possible occasion – heckling him at a Conservative Party meeting and waylaying him in the Turkish baths of their mutual club. Psmith's immediate superior in the postage department, where he is first put to work, is a Mr Rossiter, a pernickety little man, whom Psmith bemuses with a flow of words:

> 'I am now a member of the staff of this bank. Its interests are my interests. Psmith, the individual, ceases to exist, and there springs into being Psmith the cog in the wheel of the New Asiatic Bank; Psmith, the link in the bank's chain; Psmith the worker. I shall not spare myself. I shall toil with all the accumulated energy of one who, up to now, has only known what work is like from hearsay. Whose is that form sitting on the steps of the bank in the morning, waiting eagerly for the place to open? It is the form of Psmith, the Worker. Whose is that haggard, drawn face which bends over a ledger long after the other toilers have sped blithely westwards to dine at Lyons' Popular Café? It is the face of Psmith, the Worker. I tell you, Comrade Rossiter, that you have got hold of a good man. You and I together, not forgetting Comrade Jackson, the pet of the Smart Set, will toil early and late till we boost up this Postage Department into a shining model of what a Postage Department should be.'

Not surprisingly Psmith's days at the New Asiatic Bank, like Plum's in the Bank of Hong Kong and Shanghai, were numbered. And he next appeared, wildly improbably, in *Psmith Journalist* as the editor of a children's newspaper in New York called *Cosy Moments*. Here he makes drastic changes in the paper's contents, casting out such features as 'Moments of Mirth', 'Moments in the Nursery', and 'Moments with Budding Girlhood', and replacing them with articles exposing the wicked ways of racketeering New York landlords, which involves him in escapades in New York gang warfare.

Plum had intended that this should have been the last of Psmith, but some years later he was prevailed on by his step-daughter, Leonora, to whom he could refuse nothing, to write one more. And so there appeared *Leave it to Psmith* (1924), where he is to be found first seeking a job at Clarkson's Employment Agency, having just emerged from a stint in his uncle's fish business. This had been a horrendously painful experience as he recounted to a somewhat dazed Miss Clarkson:

> *To me, Miss Clarkson, from the very start, the fish business was what I can only describe as a wash-out. It nauseated my finer feelings. It got right in amongst my fibres. I had to rise and partake of a simple breakfast at about four in the morning, after which I would make my way to Billingsgate Market and stand for some hours knee-deep in dead fish of every description. A jolly life for a cat, no doubt, but a bit too thick for a Shropshire Psmith. Mine, Miss Clarkson, is a refined and poetic nature. I like to be surrounded by joy and life, and I know nothing more joyless and deader than a dead fish. Multiply that dead fish by a million, and you have an environment which only Dante could contemplate with equanimity. My uncle used to tell me that the way to ascertain whether a fish was fresh was to peer into its eyes. Could I spend the springtime of my life staring into the eyes of a dead fish? No!'*

But better things were in store for him. He was to find his way to Blandings Castle where, masquerading as a modern Canadian poet, he became involved in a plot of considerable complexity in which he was commissioned by a husband to steal (for the best of motives) his wife's diamond necklace. But also staying at the Castle and posing as literary figures and very much interested in the necklace for their own ends, was a couple of American criminals, Ed Coote and his partner, 'Smooth Lizzie', and it fell to Psmith to frustrate their evil designs. For this he was rewarded by being made Lord Emsworth's secretary in place of the odious Efficient Baxter, but then, sadly, he disappeared from the scene and was heard of no more.

Uncle Fred

One of the hottest earls who ever donned a coronet.

I don't know if you happen to know what the word 'excesses' means, but those are what he invariably commits, when on the loose.

He held it in truth with him who sings to one clear harp in divers tones that men may rise on stepping stones of their dead selves to higher things.

'Uncle Fred,' he said, speaking in a low, metallic voice, 'I don't know if you know it but you're Public Scourge Number One. You scatter ruin and devastation on every side like a ruddy sower going forth sowing. Life, liberty and the pursuit of happiness aren't possible when you're around.'

Those who lamented the sudden and complete disappearance of Psmith were compensated thirteen years later by the arrival on the scene of a character whom Plum regarded as 'a sort of elderly Psmith'. This was Frederick Altamont Cornwallis, fifth Earl of Ickenham, generally known as Uncle Fred. He arrived with a bang in one of Plum's best short stories, *Uncle Fred Flits by*, contained in *Young Men in Spats*. By then Uncle Fred was in his sixties, but 'as young as he feels which is about twenty-three':

> *In the evening of his life he still retained, together with a juvenile waistline, the bright enthusiasms and fresh, unspoiled mental outlook of a slightly inebriated undergraduate.*

Of his early life we only know by hearsay, but it had been lively. In Edwardian London he had played fast and loose and had been a notorious figure on the social scene, notably at race meetings and nightclubs, from most of which at some time he had been forcibly ejected. But this life could not last, for at that time he was not yet an Earl, only a Hon. which was, as he later recalled, a very different matter:

> *Do you know how they treat Hons., Sally? Like dogs. They have to go into dinner behind the Vice-Chancellor of the County Palatinate of Lancaster ... The only bit of sunshine in their lives is the privilege of being allowed to stand at the bar of the House of Lords during debates.*

It was necessary for him, therefore, to earn some sort of a living, which he had attempted to do in America, sometimes as a cow puncher, sometimes as a soda jerker and sometimes prospecting unsuccessfully for gold in the Mojave Desert. Now in later life a fully fledged earl, he is immured for most of the year in Ickenham Hall, where his loving but formidable wife Jane attempts to exercise some restraint on him. But all the time he yearns for London. Bishop's Ickenham he regards as 'a rural morgue'. It is in London that 'his soul can expand like a blossoming flower' and he can indulge the great passion of his life of 'spreading sweetness and light and perhaps a little joy into any life, no matter how'. Opportunities for London visits are rare, but when they do occur he makes the most of them, and when he arrives at The Drones Club, 'stepping high, wide and handsome', it always causes the greatest consternation to his nephew, Pongo Twistleton-Twistleton, who knows only too well what trouble may lie in store. There had been an incident at a greyhound stadium when the two of them were arrested and only Uncle Fred's presence of mind in giving his name and address as George Robinson of 14 Nasturtium Road, East Dulwich had prevented a scandal. And then there was the occasion, recorded in *Uncle Fred Flits By*, when on a visit to the suburbs to have a look at the changed face of the old Ickenham estates, Uncle Fred took refuge from the rain in a suburban villa, masquerading as the vet who had come to clip the claws of the parrot, with Pongo his anaesthetist. And once inside he discovered an opportunity for spreading sweetness and light by smoothing the path of true love for a young lady with a face like 'a dewy rosebud at daybreak on a June morning' and a pink young man who jellied eels for a living.

On other occasions when Uncle Fred has broken loose from his ancestral home, he is to be found impersonating a famous explorer at a country house dominated by a cantankerous ex-colonial governor (with whom, it transpired, he had once been at school and to whom he had administered six of the best with a fives bat for bullying), and at Blandings Castle pretending to be Sir Roderick Glossop, the eminent psychiatrist. In all these escapades his object was the same, that of rendering assistance to others. 'Help,' he once said, 'is a thing I am always glad to be of. I think my mother must have been frightened by a boy scout.' Usually such help meant sorting out the love affairs of the younger generation and giving advice based on his own long and varied experience. Thus to his nephew, who had become engaged (mistakenly as he thought) to a beautiful, high-minded girl:

'What you need,' he told Pongo, 'is a jolly, lively wife to take you out of yourself, the sort of wife who would set booby traps for the bishop when he came to spend the night. I don't suppose this Hermione Bostock of yours ever made so much as an apple-pie bed in her life. Send her an affectionate telegram saying you've changed your mind and it's all off.'

To another young man in love with the same girl he gave different advice. Up to then he had been 'a speechless, craven lover, shuffling his feet and looking popeyed whenever in the presence of the loved one'. To him Uncle Fred expounded the Ickenham System:

43

Diffident young shepherd and Goddess

Swiftness and decision are what is needed. Don't hesitate. Have at her. Sweep her off her feet. Take her by storm . . . I can understand your feeling a little nervous. When I saw Hermione Bostock's photograph, I was struck at once by something formidable in her face, a touch of that majestic inaccessibility which used to cramp the style of diffident young shepherds in their relations with the more dignified of the goddesses of Mount Olympus. She is what in my day would have been called a proud beauty. And that makes it all the more necessary to take a strong line from the start. Proud beauties have to be dominated . . . Where a Pongo can click by looking fragile and stammering words of endearment, you must be the whirlwind wooer, or nothing. You will have to behave like the hero of those novels, which were so popular at one time, who went about in riding breeches and were not above giving the girl of their choice a couple with a hunting crop on the spot where it would do most good.

At first the young man had been horrified by such advice, but then, stung to fury by an insult, he found himself following it (with certain modifications) and, of course, it worked.

Uncle Fred was the leading light in one short story and four novels. He never changed. To the end he was as youthful and resourceful as ever. 'Anachronistic parasite on the body of the state' though some might regard him, his capacity for spreading sweetness and light never dimmed.

45

Chapter 5

Nature abhors a vacuum . . . for many a long month his heart had been lying empty, all swept and garnished with 'Welcome' on the mat.

. . . what he had mistaken for the divine emotion before was but a pale imitation of the real thing.

Marriage is a battlefield, not a bed of roses.

It was an awfully curious thing how everything altered just after we got married.

Plum had so much enjoyed his visit to America that it was not long before he went again, and soon visiting America became part of his way of life. Not only did he find the country exciting but he was beginning to sell his work there at higher prices than in England. In 1909, on his second visit, he sold some stories to American magazines so well that he gave up his job on the *Globe* and thought of settling in America. However, he was to find that, although occasional prices might be higher, he could not obtain a regular source of income there, so for the time being he returned to England and resumed his job on the *Globe*. In England Plum was by now an established writer, but not yet a best seller. His unique style, which in time would make P. G. Wodehouse a household name, had not yet been perfected. But it was coming. 1910 was a particularly fruitful year, seeing the publication of *Psmith in the City*, surely one of his funniest books, and *A Gentleman of Leisure*, his first novel set partly in an English stately home. He was also contributing regularly to *Strand* magazine, perhaps the greatest accolade for an English writer at that time. Altogether his career was developing steadily and successfully, and his life was contented and on an even keel. But then, quite suddenly, in 1914 it was revolutionised.

In the summer Plum went on another visit to America; he landed in the country on 2nd August; two days later the First World War broke out; and at the same time Plum made the acquaintance of an English widow, Ethel Wayman, who was also on a visit to America. Two months later they were married.

At first sight it seemed a strange partnership – an attraction of opposites. Plum was shy, reclusive and unemotional; Ethel was extrovert, sociable, hyperactive and highly strung. Plum dreaded the social scene, Ethel revelled in it. But although so different they were to be married happily for sixty years, surviving some rough storms. At heart they knew they depended on each other. Plum needed an efficient, strong-minded manager, leaving him free to concentrate on his writing; Ethel needed steadiness and security. Her life until then had been tumultuous and tragic. She had never known her father, and her mother was an alcoholic so that she had been put in care. At the age of eighteen she had become pregnant and had had to make a hasty marriage to a mining engineer, Leonard Rowley, by whom she had a daughter, Leonora. He died four years later in India and soon afterwards Ethel married again, this time a tailor of the name of Wayman who went bankrupt and committed suicide. Ethel then put Leonora in a boarding school and sought a living in America as an actress in a repertory company. It was as such that she first met Plum.

Nothing is known of Plum's wooing of Ethel except that it was very brief. Plum himself never spoke of it; it was much too personal and, like most Englishmen, he dreaded talking about his inner feelings. In *Money for Nothing* two types of lover are compared, and there can be no doubt which was Plum:

> *John drew a deep breath. He was not one of those men who derive pleasure from parading their inmost feelings and discussing with others the secrets of their hearts. Hugo, in a similar situation, would have advertised his love like the hero of a musical comedy; he would have made the round of his friends, confiding in them; and, when the supply of friends had given out, would have buttonholed the gardener. But John was different. To hear his aspirations put into bald words like this made him feel as if he were being divested of most of his more important garments in a crowded thoroughfare.*

It seems likely that it was love at first sight; Plum was a great believer in this and often quoted Marlowe's line: 'Who ever loved that loved not at first sight?' And in his books most of the love matches began with the hero being stunned by his first glimpse of the heroine. At the time of his marriage Plum was thirty-two. It would seem that until then he had never been seriously in love; there had been attachments but they had evaporated; they had, as he put it, 'been but pale imitations of the real thing'. But he always expected that one day he would marry. He was not one of nature's bachelors, although his was not a deeply passionate nature.

Perhaps the nearest Plum came to describing his love occurred in *Something Fresh*, the first novel he wrote after marriage. This, though light-hearted, hinted at something deeper:

> *From his fourteenth year onward Ashe had been in love many times. His sensations in the case of Joan were neither the terrific upheaval which had caused him in his fifteenth year to collect twenty-eight photographs of the principal girl of the Theatre Royal, Birmingham, pantomime, nor the milder flame which had caused him, when at Oxford, to give up smoking for a week and try to learn by heart Sonnets from the Portuguese . . . He did not wish the station at Market Blandings to become suddenly congested with Red Indians, so that he might save Joan's life, and he did not wish to give up anything at all. But he was conscious, to the very depths of his being, that a future in which Joan did not figure would be so insupportable as not to bear considering.*

In *Something Fresh* too there may be a glimpse of Ethel in the heroine, Joan Valentine who, like her, had been through hard times:

The vision of Joan Valentine: . . . 'strong, cheerful, self-reliant, bearing herself in spite of adversity with a valiant jauntiness.'

And again:

Her eyes (were) as brightly blue as a November sky when the sun is shining on a frosty world. There was in them a little of November's cold glitter, too, for Joan had been through much in the last few years, and experience, even if it does not harden, erects a defensive barrier between its children and the world. Her eyes were eyes that looked straight and challenged . . . She looked what she was – a girl of action, a girl whom Life had made both reckless and wary, wary of friendly advances, reckless when there was a venture afoot.

Plum was to discover that marriage could make the whole difference to a man's life and that love could raise him to a higher plane; but this did not prevent him in his books from treating it flippantly:

The word is so loosely used to cover a thousand varying shades of emotion – from the volcanic passion of an Anthony for a Cleopatra to the tepid preference of a grocer's assistant for the housemaid at the second house in the High Street as opposed to the cook at the first house past the Post Office.

His love scenes are invariably low-key with much bickering and badinage. 'Words of molten passion' are referred to but never uttered. Plum's favourite treatment was to mob up the language of popular romantic fiction, such as occurred in the Nosegay Novelettes, which the less sophisticated characters in his books were always reading. And even true troubadours, whose emotions were deep and genuine, found themselves talking of the divine emotion in this overblown language. Thus Sam Marlowe in *The Girl on the Boat*:

> *I would pour out upon her the stored-up devotion of a lifetime, lay an unblemished heart at her feet and say: 'At Last!'.*

Or Joss Weatherby in *Quick Service*:

> *I dream all the time of some sweet girl who will some day come into my life like a tender goddess and gaze into my eyes and put a hand on each cheek and draw my face down to hers and whisper: 'My man!'*

Like the characters in his books, Plum concealed his own deepest feelings behind a barrier of facetiousness. He had no inclination to emulate other writers of the time who were becoming liberated from Victorian restraints and were writing of love and love-making in more explicit terms. Plum, ever the Victorian, always kept his love scenes within certain bounds; there was never anything in them 'calculated to bring the blush of shame to the cheek of modesty'. A man might kiss a girl, hold her hand, even clasp her in his arms, but no more. The facts of life were kept at a distance. At times in his books Plum seemed to show admiration for the dashing and forceful lover who relied on 'the quick smash and grab' rather than 'the honeyed word'; but it must be doubtful if he himself was one of their number. One suspects that in love-making he favoured a measure of propriety and may even have looked back nostalgically on the decorum of Victorian days as described in *The Girl on the Boat*:

> *When Samuel's grandfather had convinced himself, after a year and a half of respectful aloofness, that the emotion he felt towards Samuel Marlowe's grandmother-to-be was love, the fashion of the period compelled him to approach the matter in a roundabout way. First he spent an evening or two singing sentimental ballads, she accompanying him on the piano and the rest of the family sitting on the sidelines to see that no rough stuff was pulled. Having noted that she drooped her eyelashes and turned faintly pink when he came to the 'Thee — only thee!' bit, he felt a mild sense of encouragement, strong enough to justify him in taking her sister aside next day and asking if the object of his affections ever happened to mention his name in the course of conversation. Further pourparlers having passed with her aunt, two more sisters and her little brother, he felt the moment had arrived when he might send her a volume of Shelley, with some of the passages marked in pencil. A few weeks later he interviewed her father and obtained his consent to the paying of his addresses. And finally, after writing her a letter which began 'Madam, you will not have been insensible to the fact that for some time past you have inspired in my bosom feelings deeper than those of ordinary friendship . . .' he waylaid her in the rose garden and brought the thing off.*

In their early married life Plum and Ethel were not well off, but quite soon, with Plum's successes in the theatre, they became more affluent. But even when he had great wealth Plum wanted nothing more than to live quietly away from the social scene preferably in solitude. But this was not to Ethel's taste. She hankered after the pleasure grounds of the world – Nice, Biarritz, Monte Carlo. Parties and social occasions were the breath of life to her. She bought racehorses and gambled for high stakes, and Plum was content that she should do so. His own needs were minimal – a few pounds a week for such things as pipe tobacco and typewriter ribbons; he wanted little more. He was not, however, as uninterested in money as is sometimes supposed. He would often argue strongly with his publishers about the terms of his contracts and kept bank accounts unknown to Ethel from which at times he distributed funds to his more impecunious friends.

In most ways Ethel was the ideal wife for Plum. Practical, high-powered and well-organised, she took over completely all domestic and most financial matters and dealt with those things he found tedious and burdensome. She did not, however, always give him a smooth ride. She could be something of a tornado in the house, when he might be required to pull his weight in domestic matters and on occasions forced into unfamiliar and un-comfortable clothes to attend social functions. But she did realise how important it was for him to have time for his writing, and his readers should be grateful to her for seeing that he had as much of this, or nearly as much, as he needed. Malcolm Muggeridge, the well-known journalist and broadcaster, who became a great family friend, has given a memorable description of her:

> *She is a spirited, energetic woman, who tries as hard to be worldly-wise as Wodehouse does to be innocent; a bad sleeper, who wanders about during the night polishing tables, and planning to pull down whatever house she is living in and rebuild it nearer to her heart's desire; a mixture of Mistress Quickly and Florence Nightingale, with a bit of Lady Macbeth thrown in. I grew to love her.*[1]

When he first became engaged Plum had been apprehensive about his relationship with Ethel's daughter, Leonora, then aged nine and at school in England; but he need have had no worries. They became devoted to each other at once. Leonora was a remarkable child – lively, intelligent and full of laughter. With her Plum's shyness disappeared completely; she was perhaps the person with whom he was most completely at ease.

[1] From *Tread Softly for you Tread on my Jokes* by Malcolm Muggeridge (Collins, 1966).

Chapter 6

There's no business like show business. (Irving Berlin)

*For pure lunacy nothing can touch the musical comedy business
... In the theatre when it comes to business everything goes except
biting and gouging. (P.G.W.)*

Soon after the outbreak of the First World War Plum
presented himself, as he was required to do, for military
service, but because of poor eyesight was rejected. This
meant that he was free to remain in America and carry
on with his career as a writer, which he proceeded to do.
Most people will be glad that such a great writer was
spared the slaughter fields of France and Belgium, but
there were some who thought he might have done more
than he did to help his country at that time. Certainly
he distanced himself from the war, and there is no record
that he ever made any significant contribution to the War
Effort. There was, undeniably, a streak of escapism in
him. In his life, as in his books, the grim and unpleasant
things of the world were excluded; he would not have
written the books he did if it had been otherwise. But
such aloofness and indifference have their dangers. In
the First World War they caused only muted murmurings,

but in the Second World War, as will be seen, they were to be disastrous.

During the war years Plum continued to write novels and short stories, but was principally concerned with work for the theatre. As has been seen, he had had experience of this in England, and in the course of it had made the acquaintance of an up and coming young American composer who was to become one of the great song writers of the century – Jerome Kern. Soon after arriving in New York Plum became theatre critic of a magazine and met up with Kern again when he went to review one of his musical comedies. This meeting was to prove a turning point in his career, and indeed in the history of musical comedy. It led to a long and highly successful collaboration between himself, Kern and Guy Bolton. Guy Bolton, later to become Plum's closest friend, was having considerable success at that time writing the books for musical comedies – that is the story and the dialogue – but he did not regard himself as a lyricist. And it was here that Plum came in. During the following years the three men, working in partnership, were to pioneer a new type of musical comedy, the miniature musical. At that time the fashion was for large, lavish musicals full of glittering girls, sumptuous scenery and soloists with big names. The storyline was thin to the point of non-existence, and the soloists sang songs which may or may not have had any bearing on it. At intervals comedians appeared and 'did their own thing', and the stage was almost always full of beautiful ladies who did not necessarily have any reason for being there. They were primarily ornamental;

no great feats of singing or dancing were required of them. This was recalled by Plum in his book, *Summer Moonshine*:

> *It must be remembered that it is only in these restless modern days that the term 'chorus girl' has come to connote a small, wiry person with indiarubber legs and flexible joints, suffering, to all appearances, from an advanced form of St Vitus's Dance.*
>
> *In the era of Lady Abbott's professional career, the personnel of the ensemble were tall, stately creatures, shaped like hourglasses, who stood gazing dreamily at the audience, supporting themselves on long parasols. Sometimes they would emerge from the coma for an instant to bow slightly to a friend in the front row, but not often. As a rule they just stood statuesquely.*

And they were not even expected to dance, for

> *that word could hardly be used legitimately to describe the languid stirrings of the lower limbs which used to afflict the personnel of the ensembles of musical comedies at the conclusion of a number.*

The idea of a new type of musical comedy originated in a small New York theatre called the Princess. It was the brainchild of a large, affable lady, Elizabeth Marbury – 'dear, kindly voluminous Bessy', as Plum called her. Her idea was that musicals should be much more intimate, with only a small cast and modest scenery, but with new, original music and a strong storyline. And all songs and comedy situations should arise from the story, not, as had happened before, be put in at random.

In the event the first show on which Bolton, Wodehouse and Kern collaborated was a musical of the old style, an adaptation of a Viennese operetta to be called *Miss Springtime* and to be put on at one of New York's largest theatres. It proved highly successful, and from then on theatre agents were eager to obtain the services of the new partnership. It was not long, however, before Plum began to realise that the New York theatre scene was something of a jungle. For in their next show the partners fell into the hands of one of the sharpest operators in show business. Colonel Henry Savage was the grandson of a slave trader, and wise to every trick in the trade. Not only did the three men find themselves working extremely hard for minimal return, but they were even obliged to pay out of their own money for a performer they particularly wanted. Of Savage Plum later wrote: 'He was so crooked he could hide at will behind a spiral staircase.' During his years in the theatre Plum's dislike of theatrical agents was to intensify. In his books they are always portrayed as ignorant, devious and uncouth:

> ... *the lowest form of intelligence – with the possible exception of the limax maximus or garden slug – known to science.*
>
> *Stout whisky-nourished men who sat behind paper-littered tables smoking cigars in rooms marked 'Private'.*
>
> *He looked soft and glutinous – reptilian with a greasy soul and withered heart.*

Plum had clearly suffered much at their hands.

The partnership's second show, *Have a Heart*, proved moderately successful, and as soon as it was launched the three started working on the first of their new-style musicals for the Princess Theatre to be called *Oh, Boy!* and this was a resounding success. New York was full of their praises and more than ever theatrical agents were seeking new works from them. And the three responded heroically. During 1917 at various times Plum had no less than seven shows running on Broadway. Such success was sensational, but they were in for a rude shock. All too often in the theatre great success is followed by great failure. The trouble was, as Plum later admitted, they were taking on more than they could manage: 'We had so many irons in the fire that they put the fire out.' Three of their shows failed. New York audiences 'stayed away in droves'. And Plum was to discover what it was to have a flop on his hands – the stony silence of the audience, the rows of empty seats, a gifted and hardworking cast put out of work, and the scenery carted off to Cain's Storehouse, a grim and gloomy building where scenery from failed shows always seemed to end up.

From being the heroes of Broadway the partners had become pariahs. No one wanted to be associated with them. But not quite all: the manager of the Princess Theatre still had confidence in them; and as always, when they applied themselves to the type of musical they did best – the intimate rather than the lavish – success returned to them with the show *Oh, Lady! Lady!* in 1918.

The theatre played a vital part in Plum's career. It brought him fame and fortune and great excitement. But it is clear from what he later wrote that his feelings towards it were ambivalent: there was distaste as well as love. Auto-biographical undertones can be discerned in *A Damsel in Distress*, in which George Bevan, a highly successful composer of musical comedies, becomes disenchanted with the theatre and with musical comedy in particular – with the artificiality, the slightness of the material and the hectic and shallow way of life. And life at times could be exasperating and exceedingly arduous, especially so when the show was on tour before opening on Broadway. It was then that snags and failures came to light and had to be overcome, involving long rehearsals, lasting sometimes all through the night, in dark, decrepit rooms with everyone's nerves on edge. For the lyricist it was often necessary to write new verses or even new songs at a moment's notice. Tantrums were often thrown, usually by leading ladies. In *A Damsel in Distress* Plum recalls how they always seemed to be wanting something or complaining about something:

> *Some had kicked about their musical numbers, some about their love scenes; some had grumbled about their exit lines, others about the lines of their second-act frocks. They had kicked in a myriad differing ways – wrathfully, sweetly, noisily, softly, smilingly, tearfully, pathetically and patronisingly; but they had all kicked; with the result that woman had now become to George not so much a flaming inspiration or a tender goddess as something to be dodged – tactfully, if possible; but, if not possible by open flight.*

Producers too were liable to give trouble, suddenly deciding, maybe, that what the show needed was a troupe of jugglers or performing dogs, and that everything had to be rewritten to accommodate them. Agonising sessions were held in the watches of the night to decide what should be done about scenes which were not going well. And invariably on these occasions the favoured solution was 'to bring on the girls'. It was firmly believed by some that theatre audiences could never have too much of lovely ladies. Years later, when Plum came to write his reminiscences of the theatre, he chose as the title *Bring on the Girls*.

At the time Plum's work in the theatre was rated very highly; he was regarded as one of the best lyricists in the business. Today, however, his lyrics seem less remarkable. Unlike those of his great hero, W. S. Gilbert, they are seldom quoted. Perhaps he was at a disadvantage compared with Gilbert, who wrote the words first and then gave them to Sullivan to set to music. For Plum it was the other way round; he took a tune and then found words for it. He preferred it that way, and this in spite of the fact that he was totally unmusical. His step-daughter once wrote that he would not know the difference between Tosti's 'Farewell' and 'Red Hot Mamma'. Yet he had the knack of picking up the rhythm of a tune and getting the feel of it. Sometimes it was only necessary for someone to hum a tune to him over the telephone two or three times, and words would be forthcoming in a few days, sometimes sooner.

One example of Plum's lyrics will show that, though skilful and entertaining, they are not particularly memorable. Here are some verses of his on Napoleon:

Napoleon was a little guy:
They used to call him Shorty.
He only stood about so high.
His chest was under forty;
But when folks started talking mean,
His pride it didn't injure.
'My queen,' he'd say to Josephine,
'The thing that counts is ginger.'

He got too fat. We all know that
From portraits in the galleries.
He never seemed to learn the knack
Of laying off the calories.
But though his waist was large, he faced
And overcame all foemen.
He knew quite well it's brains that tell
And not a guy's abdomen.

Chapter 7

The morning sunshine descended like an amber showerbath on Blandings Castle.

Blandings Castle slept in the sunshine . . . Blandings Castle dozed in the twilight.

Lord Emsworth, mould-stained and wearing a deplorable old jacket, pottered into the room.

During the years 1915 to 1930, when Plum was constantly engaged in work for the theatre, he still found time for a steady stream of articles, short stories and novels; and these were having increasing success. The main breakthrough came in 1915 when the serial rights to his book, *Something Fresh* (*Something New* in America) were sold at an impressive price to the *Saturday Evening Post*, the best known and most expensive of American magazines. To become a regular contributor, or even an occasional one, was the dream of all aspiring writers. As well as initiating Plum's long connection with the magazine, *Something Fresh* was important for another reason: it was the first Blandings novel.

It was an instant success and many more were to follow;

people were entranced by the stately home, Blandings Castle, and its motley inhabitants. Many vivid descriptions were to be given of its beauty, charm and numerous idiosyncrasies. In *Summer Lightning*:

> *Blandings Castle slept in the sunshine. Dancing little ripples of heatmist played across its smooth lawns and stone-flagged terraces. The air was full of the lulling drone of insects. It was that gracious hour of a summer afternoon, midway between luncheon and tea, when Nature seems to unbutton its waistcoat and put its feet up.*

And in *Blandings Castle (The Custody of the Pumpkin)*:

> *The morning sunshine descended like an amber showerbath on Blandings Castle, lighting up with a heartening glow its ivied walls, its rolling parks, its gardens, outhouses, and messuages, and such of its inhabitants as chanced at the moment to be taking the air. It fell on green lawns and wide terraces, on noble trees and bright flowerbeds. It fell on the baggy trousers-seat of Angus McAllister, head gardener to the ninth Earl of Emsworth, as he bent with dour Scottish determination to pluck a slug from its reverie beneath the leaf of a lettuce. It fell on the white flannels of the Hon. Freddie Threepwood, Lord Emsworth's second son, hurrying across the water meadows. It also fell on Lord Emsworth himself and on Beach, his faithful butler.*

And then Blandings at night in *Heavy Weather*:

THE STORY OF HIS LIFE

Darkness had fallen on Blandings Castle, the soft, caressing darkness that closes in like a velvet curtain at the end of a summer day. Now slept the crimson petal and the white. Owls hooted in the shadows. Bushes rustled as the small creatures of the night went about their mysterious businesses. The scent of the wet earth mingled with the fragrance of stock and of wallflower. Bats wheeled against the starlit sky, and moths blundered in and out of the shaft of golden light that shone from the window of the dining room. It was the hour when men forget their troubles about the friendly board.

The occupants of Blandings Castle were an eccentric and colourful company. In the first place there was the seigneur, the ninth Earl of Emsworth, 'that amiable and bone-headed peer', who seemed to those who knew him 'to approach more nearly to the cuckoo' every time they saw him. Left to himself the Earl was a happy man. All he ever wanted to do was to sniff his roses, watch the growth of an immense pumpkin and brood over his magnificent pig, the Empress of Blandings. On a summer evening he was usually to be found in the Empress's company:

The ninth earl was down by the pigsty near the kitchen garden, draped in a boneless way over the rail of the bijou residence of Empress of Blandings, his amiable sow, twice in successive years a popular winner in the Fat Pigs class at the Shropshire Agricultural Show.

The ecstasy which always came to the vague and woollen-headed peer when in the society of this noble animal was not quite complete, for she had withdrawn for the night to a

65

The ninth earl at the pigsty

sort of covered wigwam in the background and he could not see her. But he could hear her deep, regular breathing, and he was drinking it in as absorbedly as if it had been something from the Queen's Hall conducted by Sir Henry Wood.

But all too often Lord Emsworth was not left to himself. His wife had died, but invariably one of his formidable sisters was at the Castle and ruling it with a rod of iron. This was particularly the case with Lady Constance Keeble. She was a holy terror; with arched nose and the eye of a lion-tamer and 'apt to comport herself in a manner reminiscent of Cleopatra on one of the latter's bad mornings'. And she was always forcing her brother to do things he didn't want to do – to attend to tiresome family business, to entertain unwanted guests and to become involved in family quarrels from which he longed to distance himself. There were sometimes painful occasions with everyone talking at once and poor Lord Emsworth with his 'woolly, wobbly mind which could only accommodate one thought at a time, if that', sitting miserably on the sidelines. Lord Emsworth in the library was a very different man from Lord Emsworth by the pigsty:

Sunshine, calling to all right-thinking men to come out and revel in its heartening warmth, poured in at the windows of the great library of Blandings Castle. But to Clarence, ninth Earl of Emsworth, much as he liked sunshine as a rule, it brought no cheer. His face drawn, his pince-nez askew, his tie drooping away from its stud like a languorous lily, he sat staring sightlessly before him. He looked like something that had just been prepared for stuffing by a taxidermist.

Someone else who never failed to disturb Lord Emsworth's peace of mind was his younger son, the Hon. Freddie Threepwood, 'an animated talking machine' with 'the eyes of a fish'. His had been a chequered career:

He had been expelled from Eton for breaking out at night and roaming the streets of Windsor in a false moustache. He had been sent down from Oxford for pouring ink from a second-storey window onto the Junior Dean of his college. He had spent two years at an expensive London crammer and failed to pass into the army. He had also accumulated an almost record series of racing debts, beside as shady a gang of friends, for the most part vaguely connected with the turf, as any young man of his age ever contrived to collect.

It was the greatest satisfaction to his father when Freddie married the daughter of an American dog biscuit tycoon and put three thousand miles of water between himself and Blandings. But he was always liable to return and bombard everyone he knew, including his father, with the wonders of Donaldson's Dog Joy.

The most colourful resident at the Castle was Lord Emsworth's younger brother, the Hon. Galahad Threepwood. Now in late middle age, he could look back with relish on a thoroughly misspent life among the music halls, restaurants, nightclubs and other pleasure haunts of Edwardian London. He was the one member of the family to have become famous, indeed something of a legend:

There were men in London — bookmakers, skittle sharps, jellied eels sellers on race-courses, and men like that — who would have been puzzled to have known whom you were referring to if you had mentioned Einstein, but they all knew Gally.

And yet, in spite of a riotous youth, Gally in his fifty-seventh year was as fit as a fiddle:

Everything about this Musketeer of the nineties was jaunty. It was a standing mystery to all who knew him that one who had had such an extraordinarily good time all his life should, in the evening of his life, be so superbly robust. Wan contemporaries who had once painted a gas-lit London red in his company and were now doomed to an existence of dry toast, Vichy Water and German cure resorts felt very strongly on this point. A man of his antecedents, they considered, ought by rights to be rounding off his career in a bath chair instead of flitting about the place, still chaffing head waiters as of old and calling for the wine list without a tremor.

A little cock-sparrow of a man. One of the Old Guard which dies but does not surrender. Sitting there under the cedar, he looked as if he were just making ready to go to some dance-hall when dance halls were dance-halls, from which in the quiet dawn it would take at least three waiters, two commissionaires and a policeman to eject him.

69

Eviction of the Hon. Galahad

THE STORY OF HIS LIFE

And everything he did was with such style. All around him might be in turmoil, but the Hon. Galahad's calm was never disturbed:

> *Cooled by the shade of the cedar, refreshed by the contents of the amber glass in which ice tinkled so musically when he lifted it to his lips, the Hon. Galahad, at the moment of Lord Emsworth's arrival, had achieved a Nirvana-like repose. Storms might be raging elsewhere in the grounds of Blandings Castle, but here on the lawn there was peace – the perfect unruffled peace which in this world seems to come only to those who have done nothing whatever to deserve it.*

In addition to members of the family there was too at the Castle an army of domestic servants – housemaids, parlour maids, kitchen maids, between maids, footmen, odd-job men and others. First and foremost there was Beach, the butler, massive and stately, doing little actual work, but always lending great tone:

> *One's first impression of Beach was one of tension . . . He had that strained air of being on the very point of bursting which one sees in frogs and toy balloons. Nervous and imaginative men, meeting Beach, braced themselves involuntarily, stiffening their muscles for the explosion. Those who had the pleasure of more intimate acquaintance with him soon passed this stage, just as people whose homes are on the slopes of Mount Vesuvius become immune to fear of eruptions. Beach had always looked as if an apoplectic fit was a matter of minutes away, but he never had apoplexy, and in time they came to ignore the possibility of it.*

Beach: massive and stately

Outside the Castle there was a full complement of gardeners headed by Angus McAllister, a dour Scotsman full of honesty and intelligence but 'a bit short on sweetness and light', who always kept the superb garden immaculate in spite of being 'a good deal hampered by Lord Emsworth's amateur assistance'.

Visitors to the Castle might include lunatic and violent dukes, dyspeptic American millionaires, lovelorn nieces and nephews, stray poetesses and, not infrequently, the criminal classes.

Blandings Castle was Plum's favourite setting for his stories. Altogether he wrote twelve Blandings books and was halfway through another when he died. During the sixty years which had elapsed since the first story the Castle and its occupants had hardly changed at all. Lord Emsworth, vague and forgetful, was still pottering about the rose garden and the pigsties. The Hon. Freddie was still chattering away, mainly about dog biscuits; the Hon. Galahad was as sprightly and engaging as ever; and Beach was still dispensing port and good advice in his pantry. As always the weather at Blandings was a perfect summer day and the garden was at its best. For sixty years, time had stood still at Blandings Castle. World Wars had come and gone. Moon rockets, jumbo jets, Labour governments and the permissive society had all made their impact, but not on Blandings Castle. In 1977 it was the same as it had been in 1915.

Chapter 8

Bertie Wooster

'A vapid and frivolous wastrel ... A spineless invertebrate.'
(Aunt Agatha)

'A cross between an orgy scene in the movies and some low form
of pond life.' (Aunt Dahlia)

'Mr Wooster has a heart of gold, but is mentally negligible.'
(Jeeves)

'Providence looks after the chumps of this world, and personally
I'm all for it.' (Bertie Wooster)

The origins of Bertie Wooster and Jeeves are not
altogether clear. They were foreshadowed in a story Plum
wrote in 1914, *Extricating Young Gussie*, in which there
appeared a somewhat half-witted young man about town
with a manservant called Jeevons. Jeeves (named after a
professional cricketer) made his first appearance the
following year in a story in the *Saturday Evening Post*, *The
Man with Two Left Feet*. In this he had only a minor role
and attracted little attention. It was not until 1923 with

74

the publication of *The Inimitable Jeeves* that they both became national figures.

Many opprobrious things can be said of Bertie Wooster, and his Aunt Agatha said plenty, but 'mindless', 'frivolous', 'obsolete relic of an exploded feudal system' though he may be, few characters have given the world so much entertainment.

Little is told of Bertie's immediate family and background. His mother and father both died when he was young and are hardly ever mentioned. But we do know that the Woosters were a family of ancient lineage. A *sieur de Wocestre* came over with William the Conqueror and was said to have been 'very pally' with him. And later Wocestres fought at the battles of Crecy and Agincourt, 'and what's more did dashed well in them'. Bertie used to remind himself of this when called on to perform some daring deed and when he was in conflict with Jeeves. A few miscellaneous facts have emerged about Bertie's childhood. We are told that he had a nanny called Hogg who suffered from flatulence and to whom Bertie once administered 'a juicy one over the top-knot with a porringer'. We are told too that he wore Little Lord Fauntleroy suits, attended dancing classes and was made to do recitations, notably of *Ben Battle* and *The Charge of the Light Brigade*. Later we hear of him as a choirboy and boy scout and winning a prize for Scripture and flower arranging at his prep school. We know nothing of his time at Eton and Cambridge, only that he got a blue for rackets and after a Bump Supper rode naked round the quad, singing comic songs and insisting that he was a mermaid and wanting to dive into the college

A Worcester forebear going in to battle

Bertie after a bump supper

fountain and play a harp. One would like to have heard more of these exploits.

Grown to man's estate, Bertie led what some would consider an ideal existence. With all the money needed to keep him from doing a day's work, single and with no family ties and with Jeeves to attend to his personal needs, he seemed to be free to do what he liked. But even for Bertie life was not all pleasure. In the first place there were his aunts. In particular Aunt Agatha – she who resembled nothing so much as 'a well-bred vulture' and who 'eats broken bottles and wears barbed wire next to the skin'. To her Bertie was an imbecile and an idler, 'a useless blot on the fabric of society', who needed to be chivvied and goaded and generally kept up to the mark. Above all he needed to be married off to some high-powered, serious-minded girl who would improve him and 'mould' him. Left to himself, Bertie, who was nothing if not malleable, might have succumbed to some such harridan, but God and Jeeves watched over him and such a fate was avoided. And looking at some of the females involved this was indeed a deliverance.

Someone once remarked that if all the girls whom Bertie had once been engaged to were lined up, they would stretch from Hyde Park Corner to Piccadilly Circus. But there are two or three who stand out egregiously.

There is, for example, Florence Craye, 'with a wonderful profile but steeped to the gills in serious purpose and reading books on such subjects as idiopsychological ethics'. And making Bertie read them too. Like all Wodehouse beautiful women, Florence was of a compelling and imperious disposition. Jeeves described her as being 'of

Aunt Agatha, a well bred vulture

a highly determined and arbitrary temperament'. Bertie put it more simply: 'It was never certain when she might erupt'.

And then there was Honoria Glossop, 'built on the lines of the Albert Hall' and full of modern, enlightened thought. When she spoke it was always 'as if she were competing against a high wind'. And her laugh was like 'waves breaking on a stern and rock-bound coast'. With her Bertie would have had little peace; her energy was terrifying:

> One of those dashed large, brainy, strenuous, dynamic girls who, while at Cambridge, had not only enlarged her brain to the most frightful extent, but had also gone in for every kind of sport and developed the physique of a middleweight catch-as-can wrestler. She may even have boxed for the University.

Bertie described her as 'an Act of God'.

Perhaps worst of all was Madeline Bassett, 'this preeminent bit of bad news'. Like the others 'with governess blood in her', but in addition 'a droopy, soupy, sentimental exhibit with melting eyes and cooing voice and the most extraordinary views on such things as stars and rabbits'. Bertie recalls her telling him once that rabbits were gnomes in attendance on the Fairy Queen and that the stars were God's daisy chains, and that every time a fairy blew its wee nose, a baby was born.

Like W. S. Gilbert Plum often made fun of large, draconian ladies, but he did it less cruelly. Gilbert mocked them mercilessly, taunting them with their fading charms

Honoria Glossop, built on the lines of the Albert Hall

Madeline Bassett and God's daisy chains

and spreading figures. Plum was more gentle; he usually allowed them to be beautiful and, in some ways, kindly. It was their bossiness and heartiness which he ridiculed.

Besides his aunts and potential wives there were others too who intruded into Bertie's peaceful way of life. There were his friends. Like himself few of these were workers but men 'full of good cheer and blitheringness', circulating mainly in the neighbourhood of the Drones Club. Almost always one of them was in some sort of a scrape, and his first notion would be to come to Bertie, or more particularly to Jeeves, for help and advice. And Bertie, being kind-hearted and a soft touch, never failed to do what he could for him. Often this landed him in fearful situations such as singing 'Sonny Boy' at a 'clean, bright entertainment' in an East End boy's club, or creating a diversion at a fashionable girls' school by dropping bricks through a conservatory roof, or stealing a village policeman's uniform so that he could attend a local fancy dress ball. So long as Bertie followed Jeeves's advice, all went well, but sometimes he acted on his own initiative, and this invariably caused mayhem, so much so that on one occasion his Aunt Dahlia, normally well disposed towards him, gave full vent to her feelings:

'I was trying to think who you reminded me of. Somebody who went about strewing ruin and desolation and breaking up homes which, until he came along, had been happy and peaceful. Attila is the man. It's amazing,' she said, drinking me in once more. 'To look at you, one would think you were just an ordinary sort of amiable idiot – certifiable, perhaps, but quite harmless. Yet, in reality, you are a worse scourge

than the Black Death. I tell you, Bertie, when I contemplate you I seem to come up against all the underlying sorrow and horror of life with such a thud that I feel as if I had walked into a lamppost.'

In the end, of course, when affairs were at their worst, Bertie would have to call in Jeeves, who never failed to find the matter 'susceptible of adjustment'.

Bertie was also landed in trouble on occasions by his love of practical jokes ('practical pleasantries' as Jeeves called them). Apple-pie beds, giant squirts, luminous rabbits and long prongs for puncturing people's hot water bottles (and invariably the wrong people's) – all of these had great appeal to Bertie. But they confirmed the belief held by some that he was mentally defective and ought to be certified.

In fairness it must be said of Bertie Wooster that he was a peaceful, law-abiding citizen; he was no tearaway. It is true he did once find himself in the dock owing to getting 'sozzled' on Boat Race night and attempting to remove a policeman's helmet. But this was not his usual form. He did not live recklessly and his private life was impeccable. He could claim with justice that he was 'a respectable bachelor whose licence has never been so much as endorsed'.

Today it is difficult to believe that anyone at all like Bertie Wooster ever existed. But at the time Plum was growing up there were those who were similar – the Knuts or Piccadilly Johnnies, as they were called, well-to-do men-about-town who drifted around the West End, in and out of establishments not unlike the Drones

Club, and not often doing anything that could be called work. But Bertie Wooster was certainly not, as some foreigners imagined, the archetypal English gentleman of that period.

Plum had great affection for Bertie Wooster, and some people think there is more of Plum himself in Bertie than in any other of his characters. But there are basic differences. Plum, unlike Bertie, was unsociable and had no taste for bright city life; he hated clubs, never went to parties unless he had to and found smart restaurants alarming. And, of course, he was a hard worker. The only day's work Bertie is ever known to have done is to have written an article for his Aunt Dahlia's magazine, *Milady's Boudoir*, on what the well dressed man is wearing; and most of this was done by Jeeves. Plum, on the other hand, was never happy unless he was working. He may have written about the idle rich, but he himself was certainly not of their number.

Jeeves

'The man's a genius. From the collar upwards he stands alone.'

'If I had half Jeeves's brain I should have a stab at being prime minister or something.'

'Jeeves,' he went on emotionally, 'you must have that brain of yours pickled and presented to some national museum . . . when you've done with it, of course.'

It has been seen that Jeeves's entrance into literature, like all his entrances, was unobtrusive, but he soon made his presence felt. From being a colourless attendant, he became not only an impeccable manservant but also a source of all wisdom and his master's guide and mentor. His knowledge seemed infinite: he was well versed in the great works of literature and was a student of philosophy, giving measured judgement on Nietzsche and Spinoza. In addition he was fully informed on such matters as racing form, men's fashions and society gossip. Well might Bertie have wondered that with such brainpower Jeeves should be content with his lot as a 'gentleman's personal gentleman'; but such seemed to be the case, and he showed no signs of aspiring to higher things.

In *Carry On Jeeves* (1925) Jeeves displayed his powers the moment he arrived at the Wooster residence. Bertie at the time was feeling the effects of 'a rather cheery little supper' he had had the night before and was suffering agonies. Jeeves took in the situation at once and produced an instant cure:

'If you would drink this, sir,' he said, with a kind of bedside manner, rather like the royal doctor shooting the bracer into a sick prince. 'It's a little preparation of my own invention. It is the Worcester Sauce that gives it its colour. The raw egg makes it nutritious. The red pepper gives it its bite. Gentlemen have told me they have found it extremely invigorating after a late evening.'

I would have clutched at anything that looked like a lifeline that morning. I swallowed the stuff. For a moment I felt as if somebody had touched off a bomb inside the old

Jeeves, grave and unperturbable

bean and was strolling down my throat with a lighted torch, and then everything seemed suddenly to get all right. The sun shone in through the window; birds twittered in the tree-tops; and, generally speaking, hope dawned once more.

'You're engaged!' I said, as soon as I could say anything.

Jeeves lost no time in taking charge. In the first weeks of his employment he gave away to an under-gardener one of Bertie's suits which he considered vulgar, and took steps to break off Bertie's engagement to the terrible

Florence Craye. It would not, he felt, have been a suitable alliance. And besides, it was his experience that when a wife comes in at the front door, a valet goes out at the back. His miraculous powers soon became evident; and these showed themselves not only in his mental prowess but also in his physical attributes. His movements were a wonder. When he moved anywhere Bertie said that he 'oozed' or 'shimmered' or 'floated' (unlike Bertie and his friends who 'toddled' or 'biffed' or 'blew'). And when he appeared in a room it was as if by magic:

Jeeves doesn't have to open doors. He's like one of those birds in India who bung their astral bodies about, the chaps, I mean, who having gone into thin air in Bombay, reassemble the parts and appear two minutes later in Calcutta.

The power of Jeeves's eye was something Bertie Wooster constantly remarked on:

To the best of my knowledge Jeeves has never encountered a charging rhinoceros, but should this contingency occur, I have no doubt that the animal, meeting his eye, would check itself in mid-stride, roll over and lie purring with its legs in the air.

At all times Jeeves's manners and appearance were faultless; he was never put out and never showed any kind of emotion. When on duty he considered it improper even to smile, although there was sometimes 'a kind of paternal muscular spasm about the mouth which was the nearest he ever came to it'. Otherwise, as Bertie recalls, 'he wore a mask, preserving throughout the quiet stolidity of a stuffed moose'. When Bertie recounted some fearful calamity to him, his invariable reply was: 'Most disturbing, sir.' And when a character called J. Washburn Stoker threatened 'to break his damned neck', he was as impassive as ever, merely replying that this was 'a little extreme, sir, surely'. Of course, a moment later Mr Stoker had been completely overawed and was treating Jeeves with the greatest veneration.

Discreet and imperturbable though he may have been, there were, nevertheless, certain things which distressed Jeeves greatly, and on which he could not remain silent.

Jeeves and the rhinoceros

This was particularly the case in matters of dress. He was horrified when Bertie wore what he considered vulgar and unsuitable clothes. Usually Bertie allowed himself to be guided by Jeeves, but occasionally he took a line of his own and went overboard with some outrage like a scarlet cummerbund, or a glaringly loud suit of check plus-fours, or a white dinner jacket with brass buttons. Jeeves was appalled by such things and felt obliged respectfully but firmly to protest. At first Bertie was inclined to resist, as in the case of the Old Etonian spats:

> For the last day or so there had been a certain amount of coolness in the home over a pair of jazz spats which I had dug up while exploring in the Burlington Arcade. Some dashed brainy cove, probably the chap who invented those coloured cigarette cases, had recently had the rather topping idea of putting out a line of spats on the same system. I mean to say, instead of the ordinary grey and white, you can now get them in your regimental or school colours. And, believe me, it would have taken a chappie of stronger fibre than I am to resist the pair of Old Etonian spats which had smiled up at me from inside the window. I was inside the shop, opening negotiations, before it had even occurred to me that Jeeves might not approve. And I must say he had taken the thing a bit hardly. The fact of the matter is, Jeeves, though in many ways the best valet in London, is too conservative. Hide-bound, if you know what I mean, and an enemy to progress.

Needless to say soon afterwards the offending spats were burned.

Public demand for Bertie Wooster and Jeeves was to prove insatiable, and Plum did his best to satisfy it. Altogether he wrote ten novels and four collections of short stories about them over a period of nearly sixty years. During that time many world-shattering events might have occurred and the face of the country changed completely, but not Bertie Wooster and Jeeves. Like Blandings Castle, they remained in a time capsule.

Chapter 9

The secret of writing is to go through your stuff till you come to something you think particularly good and then cut it out.

If there is one thing that wakes the fiend which sleeps in all of us, it is getting stuck in the big chapter of a sunny and optimistic novel full of whimsical humour and gentle pathos.

By the early 1920s Plum had become one of the most highly paid and successful writers of the time – and these included such giants as Rudyard Kipling, Conan Doyle and H. G. Wells. Far off were the days when he was 'having the dickens of a job keeping the wolf the right side of the door'. Now work was pouring in on every side. Magazine editors were vying for the serial rights of his latest novel; theatre managers, English and American, were constantly seeking his services, as also later were the moguls of Hollywood. In 1922 he wrote to a friend: 'I have now contracted to finish a novel, six short stories and a musical show by the end of October [four months later]. It all helps to pass the time.'

Few people have been less affected by fame than Plum; there was never the least sign that it had gone to his head. He remained exactly the same as he had always been – kindly, courteous, withdrawn, naïve and unworldly. His kindliness was noted by everyone who knew him. He was never heard to say anything cruel or malicious, and it pained him to hurt anyone. To avoid this he sometimes went to extraordinary lengths, as when he made the excuse to someone he did not want to meet that he was going into the country, and then felt obliged actually to go into the country lest the person find out that he was being fobbed off.

Frances Donaldson, who has written a biography of Plum and who met him often at this time, recalls that he was 'large, smiling and speechless'. It seems that when in company the man whose books had brought laughter to millions became tongue-tied and awkward and seldom laughed or made a joke. In his books Plum wrote of parties where there was 'a flow of merry quip and flashing badinage', but on such occasions that he attended there were no contributions from him. In some there might be 'the spirit of mirth incarnate', but Plum soon became uncomfortable and restless, and usually took the first opportunity to slip away.

Plum's writing had indeed taken over his life. He was never so contented as when he was shut up alone in a sparsely furnished room with his battered old typewriter, a supply of pipe tobacco and, perhaps, a dictionary of quotations. There were a few other things he enjoyed doing but not many. He liked an occasional round of golf, loved going to watch Dulwich playing rugby and was always glad to be taking his dogs for a walk. Like many shy people Plum had a passion for dogs, particularly Pekingeses. These fascinated him and ordered his life: if they wanted to go for a walk he took them for one; if they weren't feeling like it he walked round the garden while they sat in the middle and watched; and they were even allowed to disturb him when he was working. 'Have you ever seen a man,' he wrote, 'in the thrall of a female Pekingese? Can't call his soul his own.'

One of Plum's favourite relaxations was writing long, light-hearted letters to his step-daughter, Leonora. With her there were no barriers. He wrote to her in the language he loved – childish, facetious, at times absurd (as, for example, when Leonora became engaged to be married, he wrote that Wink and Boo, his two pekes, must be bridesmaids at her wedding, carrying her train in their mouths). The letters were full of schoolboy slang of his own era, by that time long out of date; things were described as 'ripping', 'an awful fag' and 'awful rot'. And Leonora was addressed with a fantastic collection of names such as 'darling angel Snorkie', 'old bean', 'old fright', and 'old scream'. But Plum's deep affection for her was strongly evident. When she was away at school he longed for her return. He was even prepared, although it required all his courage, to visit her at school. On these occasions he was a most unorthodox visitor. Once on the day of his arrival some of the girls were amazed to see a middle-aged man, dressed more or less like a tramp, trundling up the drive on a battered old bicycle which he then dismounted and hid behind a bush. Such was Plum's fear of the headmistress, with her steely look and stiff whalebone collar, that that was as far as he was prepared to go. Leonora would have to meet him there. Later, in one of his short stories, Bertie Wooster finds himself at a girls' school where he is presented as a well-known novelist.

Plum and the peke, a battle of wills

He is called on by the headmistress to address the young ladies with 'something brave and helpful and stimulating', but can only stutter and blink and start to tell a story about a chorus girl and a stockbroker. One would like to think that this had some autobiographical echoes.

The ten years after the First World War were the most successful of Plum's career; they were certainly the most productive. During that time he wrote seventeen books and had a part in writing twelve musical comedies for the stage, collaborating with such great names as George Gershwin, Jerome Kern and Irving Berlin. At one time there were a dozen or so companies with shows of his on Broadway or on the road. The great American showman, Florenz Ziegfeld, thought very highly of his

Plum keeping a low profile at a girls' school

work, not only because of its quality but also because of the incredible speed with which it was produced. He was forever sending Plum page-long telegrams requiring him to come at once to rewrite or touch up one of his productions. This could be very profitable: on one occasion, after a show had been rewritten several times, only a few lines written by Plum remained, but he was still given credit as one of the authors and continued to draw his agreed percentage from the box office takings.

Inevitably his work on both sides of the Atlantic involved Plum in much travelling. Left to himself he would have kept this to a minimum, as he had little love for it. But Ethel adored it and was always on the move from one place to another. She was also a frequent visitor to racecourses and had some success as a racehorse owner (Plum called her 'the curse of the turf'). Plum was very tolerant of her activities so long as he was not involved in them himself. But on occasions he was forced to get out of the well-worn clothes he loved and deck himself out in dress suit, top hat, even spats, in order to attend some function. During these years Plum and Ethel were rarely in one place for long at a time. London, Paris, New York, Cannes ('of all the poisonous, foul, ghastly places') and Harrogate ('not such a bad old spot') were some of the places they were to be found in the grandest hotels. On one occasion they took a large, fashionable house in Mayfair with a retinue of ten or more domestic staff. They even rented an English stately home, Hunstanton Park in Norfolk which, like many English stately homes at that time, was falling down; nearly two-thirds of it were unusable, but there was still quite a lot left and it included rolling park lands, a rose garden and a moat.

Later it was used as a model for Rudge Hall in *Money for Nothing*, where the moat is described:

> *The moat proper was a narrow strip of water which encircled the Hall and had been placed there by the first Carmody in the days when householders believed in making things difficult for their visitors. With the gradual spread of peace throughout the land its original purposes had been forgotten, and later members of the family had broadened it and added to it and tinkered with it and sprinkled it with little islands with the view of converting it into something resembling as nearly as possible an ornamental lake.*

Plum always loved to dwell on the scenery in English country houses. In *The Girl on the Boat* he described the atmosphere at Windles Hall:

> *The morning sunlight fell pleasantly on the garden of Windles, turning it into the green and amber Paradise which Nature had intended it to be. A number of the local birds sang melodiously in the undergrowth at the end of the lawn, while others, more energetic, hopped about the grass in quest of worms. Bees, mercifully ignorant that, after they had worked themselves to the bone gathering honey, the proceeds of their labour would be collared by idle humans, buzzed industriously to and fro and dived head foremost into flowers. Winged insects danced sarabands in the sunshine. In a deckchair under the cedar tree Billie Bennett, with a sketching-block on her knee, was engaged in drawing a picture of the ruined castle . . . In the distant stable yard, unseen but audible, a boy in shirt sleeves was washing the car and singing as*

much as a treacherous memory would permit of a popular sentimental ballad.

It is agreeable to think of Plum in these splendid surroundings, rambling around, vaguely and dreamily, in the manner of Lord Emsworth – even though he was forced by Ethel into a suit of uncharacteristic plus-fours. But it is possible he was not altogether at ease there. Was he, perhaps, thinking of himself when he wrote of a character in *Money for Nothing*:

> *On the contrary, a place like Rudge Hall afflicted his town-bred nerves. Being in it seemed to him like living in the first act of an old-fashioned comic opera. He always felt that at any moment a band of villagers and retainers might dance out and start a drinking chorus.*

There were signs too that his association with a stately home made Plum realise that times had changed and things weren't what they used to be for owners of large landed properties:

> *When the first Carmody settled in Rudge he had found little to view with alarm. Those were the days when churls were churls, and a scurvy knave was quite content to work twelve hours a day, Saturdays included, in return for a little black bread and an occasional nod of approval from his overlord. But in the twentieth century England's peasantry has degenerated. Modern sons of the soil expect coddling. Their roofs leak, and you have to mend them, their walls fall down and you have to build them up; their lanes develop holes and you have to restore*

the surface, and all this runs into money. The way things were shaping, felt Mr Carmody, in a few years a landlord would be expected to pay for the repairs of his tenants' wireless sets.

With constant switches of scene it was fortunate that Plum had an extraordinary capacity for adapting himself to wherever he happened to be, and so great was his concentration that he was able to do his writing almost anywhere – in a train, hotel bedroom, a ship's cabin, even in a punt on the moat at Hunstanton Hall. There were places where he worked better than at others – Harrogate and Hunstanton Hall were good, London and Paris bad – and he liked his workroom to be simple. On one occasion in London Ethel set up for him a superb study with book-lined walls, leather armchairs and antique furniture. But Plum, after thanking her for it, said he would prefer to work in a bedroom with a plain kitchen table, hardback chair and ancient typewriter. This typewriter had become for Plum something of a sacred relic. Although frequently breaking down and requiring an endless supply of spare parts, he refused to part with it, saying he could never get used to any other. No typewriter has ever been so much repaired. Eventually it had to be replaced but only after twenty-four years and several million words of best-selling novels – an historic typewriter if ever there was one.

Reading Plum's works, one might well think that writing for him was effortless and straightforward; the sentences flow so easily, the words and phrases are always so apt. But it is the mark of genius to make the difficult seem simple. Certainly there was nothing painless about writing for Plum; we know from his letters what anguish it caused him. Sometimes words came in a rush and he could write as many as twenty-five pages a day; but more often they would not come at all, and when they did, they were wrong and had to be rewritten. It was rare that any of his books came out right the first time. Usually they had to be revised endlessly and almost always heavily cut. In one of them, appropriately named *Heavy Weather*, he needed to write 250 pages before he got the first 100 pages right. And there was another (*Uncle Fred in the Springtime*) sweated out after great effort, but at last, as he thought, all right, which was returned to him by the *Saturday Evening Post* because it could not be divided up easily into weekly serials. It was necessary to rewrite it again, but even then it would not do because it was found that the new version did not fit the pictures that had been done, and so further last-minute changes had to be made and sent in over the telephone.

Even when he was an established writer with a world-wide reputation one of Plum's books was returned to him by his publisher because it was over-length. Other famous writers in such a situation might have thrown a tantrum and refused to cut a word, but Plum had the humility to realise that the publisher was right, and set to work to cut 25,000 words. No one knew better than Plum the dangers of being too long-winded. He was frequently warning fellow authors about this. 'I believe that over-longness is the worst fault in writing,' he once wrote, and: 'Isn't it odd how one can spoil a story by being too leisurely in telling it?' And again, somewhat ruefully: 'I sometimes think the secret of writing is to go through your stuff till you come to something you think particularly good and then cut it out.' Plum's unique skill as a writer lay not so much in a flow of inspiration as in his ability to look at his work dispassionately, to cut and rewrite where necessary, and to persevere with a story even when he was bored to death with it and had come to dislike all the characters in it intensely. According to Plum only one of his books came pouring out in a rush, *Thank You, Jeeves* – surely not one of his best.

Something that always surprised Plum was the way in which his books appealed to so many different types of reader. He imagined that his readers were, like himself, unsophisticated and with no great pretensions intellectually. But he had many great enthusiasts among scholars and eminent men of letters. Perhaps his greatest admirers were from the ranks of his fellow authors who appreciated keenly not only his use of words but also the master craftsmanship with which he shaped his stories. Certainly this was something to which Plum attached great importance, and he spent many hours weaving and interweaving plots and sub-plots. Actually, as he himself admitted, his books did not have many different plots; most were variations on a few basic themes; and he once showed some annoyance with J. B. Priestley for pointing this out:

> *Priestley, however, was the worst of all, because he analysed me, blast him, and called attention to the thing I try to hush up – viz that I have only got one plot and produce it once a year with variations. I wish to goodness novelists wouldn't review novels.*

Fortunately, however, Plum's supply of variations were numerous and brilliant and were always pieced together with consummate skill. On the subject of the construction of a novel, Plum had this advice for his friend and fellow writer, William Townend:

> *I think the success of every novel depends largely on one or two high spots. The thing to do is to say to yourself: 'Which are my big scenes?' And then get every drop of juice out of them.*

It was very important too in novels, as in plays, that the main characters should have a proper build-up and be included in all the main scenes.

> *The absolute cast-iron good rule, I'm sure, in writing a story is to introduce all your characters as early as possible – especially if they are going to play important parts later.*

But most important and fundamental was to know what sort of novel you wanted to write. In Plum's view there were two main sorts:

> *. . . one is mine, making the thing a sort of musical comedy without music and ignoring real life altogether; the other is going right deep down into life and not caring a damn. The ones that fail are the ones where the writer loses his nerve and says: 'My God! I can't write this. I must tone it down.'*

Plum was always generous with help to writers less successful than himself. He had learned the technique of writing the hard way – through constant practice and much trial and error. But he was always ready to pass on what he had learned to others. And it was not only with advice and encouragement: often it was with financial aid as well.

Chapter 10

It isn't half such a crazy place as they make out. I know two or three people in Hollywood that are part sane.

And if you aren't getting divorced yourself, there's always one of your friends is, and that gives you something to chat about in the long evenings.

As one of the most successful writers of the day it was inevitable that Plum should come under pressure from the film-makers of Hollywood to put his talents at their disposal. The film industry was then at the height of its prosperity and money was flowing freely; it seemed that the great film magnates didn't mind what they spent to get what they wanted. Several tempting offers had already been made to Plum, but at first he was unwilling to commit himself for too long; and he had been one of the few people to say no to the great Hollywood tycoon, Sam Goldwyn. However, in 1930 Ethel took a hand in the matter and negotiated on his behalf a highly paid contract.

Plum must have cut a bizarre figure in Hollywood – a shambling, middle-aged Englishman in tatty old clothes among the glittering stars and bright-eyed young hopefuls who gathered there from all over the world. In a city where everyone, even waitresses and errand boys, went to work by car, Plum insisted on walking. And in a society where it was the object of everyone to give and attend as many parties as possible, Plum's one idea was to avoid them. Ethel, of course, was in her element. She arrived after Plum and immediately threw herself into the social scene, entertaining on a grand scale with parties lasting all night. Plum tried hard to avoid these, but he did not always succeed, although he usually managed to escape before they came to an end.

If to Hollywood Plum seemed something of an oddity, Hollywood to Plum seemed a complete madhouse. Apart from the flamboyance, vulgarity and extravagance of the inhabitants, Plum was baffled by his conditions of employment. He simply could not believe that he was being paid so much money to do so little work. On arrival he had expected that, as a world famous novelist and playwright, he would be commissioned to do a film of his own, but instead he was given a script on which six writers had already worked and asked to touch it up. This he did fairly quickly, changing a few lines of dialogue here and adding a few of his own there. Then for a long time he had nothing to do; but was eventually put to work on a musical film to be called *Rosalie*. With his long experience of musical stage shows he considered himself well qualified for this and worked hard at it and thought he had made a good job of it. However, when it was finished he was told that musical films were now out of fashion and that *Rosalie* was to be shelved. From then on no more work was given to him and he spent the rest of his contract writing his own books. Plum was dismayed at the fate of *Rosalie*, but it is possible he had a suspicion that the real reason for it being shelved was not that musical films were out of fashion but that he had not got it right; he had not mastered the art of film-making and did not realise how different this was from writing for the theatre.

Plum was never happy in Hollywood. He had little in common with the golden men and women whose faces and figures were being flashed onto cinema screens all over the world. And he had a strong antipathy to film producers, finding them even more objectionable than theatrical producers. In his books they were always represented as crude, ignorant, overweight men, 'lacking the more delicate sensibilities' and 'whose buttons always seemed to be creaking beneath the strain of their duties'.

Considering what a gentle and inoffensive character Plum was, it is remarkable how, on occasions during his life, he was to find himself at the centre of storms. One such occasion developed suddenly just before he left Hollywood. His studio bosses, little knowing what the consequences would be, arranged for him to give an interview to a newspaper reporter. In the course of this Plum expressed his bewilderment that during his contract Metro-Goldwyn-Mayer had paid him a very large sum of money and then given him no work of any importance. Although this remark might not seem particularly inflammatory, in the event it caused an uproar. For, unknown to Plum, an explosive situation had been developing in Hollywood. In recent years money for film-making had been almost unlimited. So great had been the demand for films all over the world and so vast the profits from them that the banks had not minded how much money they poured into them. The result had been colossal extravagance of which Plum's experience was only one example. However, the banks were beginning to become aware of the situation and to question the way in which money was being spent. And so Plum's off-the-cuff remarks, coming at that particular moment, had the effect of bringing the matter to the boil, and Plum found himself in the midst of heated controversy. In some quarters, notably MGM, he became highly unpopular, and it seemed likely that he and Hollywood had parted company for ever.

Such, however, was not to be the case. For, five years later, in 1936 Plum was back there again, once more at an enormous salary and once more with little to do. To make the situation even more grotesque the first assignment he was given was to revise and embellish the musical film he had worked on before – *Rosalie*. And once again nothing was to come of it. It had become evident that Plum's genius as a writer did not extend to the cinema, and no one realised this more clearly than Plum himself. In a letter to a friend at the time he wrote: 'Lay off old pop Wodehouse is the advice I would give to any studio that wants to get on in the world. There is no surer road to success.'

Chapter 11

*He did down the income tax authorities – the dream of every
red-blooded man. Income Tax assessors screamed with joy when
forwarding Schedule D to his address.*

*Vir lepidissime, facetissime, venustissime . . . ego autoritate mea
et totius Universitatis admitto ad gradum Doctoris in Litteris
honoris causa (Vice-Chancellor of Oxford University)*

Ever since his days in the Hongkong and Shanghai Bank,
Plum had often professed that finance was a closed book
to him and that he had a soul above it. But this was not
entirely the case. He might seem to be vague and
indifferent but in fact he kept a shrewd eye on his finances
and seldom let a profitable opportunity pass by. Under
a mask of naive unworldliness he was capable of driving
a hard bargain. When he wrote half in jest to the editor
of the *Saturday Evening Post* that he was 'so intensely
spiritual that money meant nothing' to him (even though
at the same time asking that the royalty on his latest novel
be doubled) he was not being candid.

One aspect of Plum's finances that was to cause him
endless anguish was the matter of income tax. Later in
life, when his troubles were at their peak, he was to be

accused of shirking income tax; but this was not so. Like most citizens he disliked paying it and sought to minimise it and occasionally made jocular remarks about it (like the ones quoted above); but he did not deliberately do the taxman down, although he was often badly advised and ineptly served.

The Wodehouse tax affairs were exceedingly complicated. For a very high earner, travelling incessantly and earning money in different parts of the world, they could hardly have been more so. As the law stood at that time there was no relief from double taxation: one was liable for tax both in one's country of residence as well as in the country in which the money had been earned. As a result the rates were often confiscatory. Plum and Ethel realised early on that the management of their taxation had to be delegated and in 1924 a company, known as Jeeves Dramatics Incs, was set up for that purpose. Unfortunately, however, it proved to be grossly incompetent and failed to make tax returns for three years (1926–1928). In time, of course, tax authorities in both England and America became aware of what was going on, and in 1932 made exorbitant demands. These would always have been difficult to meet but were especially so because much of the money which should have been put aside for them had been used by Ethel for speculation on the Stock Exchange, and with the coming of the Wall Street Crash of 1929 most of the shares she had bought became almost valueless.

The situation might have been critical and was only redeemed by Plum's continued high earnings and the winning of a law suit in America which was followed by tax demands being greatly reduced. Plum's losses, however, had been considerable – perhaps as much as $150,000 – but, strangely, this did not seem to distress him greatly. There was enough left for his own modest requirements, and he became fired with an incentive to work harder and make good his losses. He wrote to a friend:

> *We always did have too much money and a nest egg of about 350,000 quid in gilt edged securities is as much as anybody could want. In some ways I am not sorry this income tax business has happened . . . I now can spit on my hands and start sweating again, feeling that it really matters when I make a bit of money.*

In 1935 the Wodehouses decided to settle in France. This was partly to minimise their tax liabilities in England and America and partly because of the law requiring that all dogs brought into England from abroad should be put into quarantine for a certain time. It was unthinkable to Plum and Ethel that this should happen to their beloved pekes, and quite a compelling consideration in their choice of France was that there were no quarantine laws there. And so they bought a house in Le Touquet. It does not appear that in making this choice Plum was motivated particularly by a great love of France. Like most Englishmen he enjoyed French food and wine and an occasional flutter in a French casino. But there is no evidence that he was interested in French art or literature or in the French way of life. Although he was to live in France for nine out of the next twelve years, he remained stolidly English in his ways and never had more than a smattering of the French language. He must surely have been thinking of himself when he wrote in *The Luck of the Bodkins*:

> *Into the face of the young man who sat on the terrace of the Hotel Magnifique at Cannes there had crept a look of furtive shame, the shifty, hangdog look which announces that an Englishman is about to talk French.*

The great advantage of Le Touquet, apart from being an attractive place, was that it was only a short journey from England, and this was important to the Wodehouses, as Leonora had recently married an Englishman and was living in Kent. In the years just before the Second World War Plum and Ethel made several visits to England, but usually separately, as it would be upsetting for their dogs to be left alone with a French maid. In 1939 they went for a special occasion: Plum was to be made a Doctor of Letters by Oxford University.

It was a constant source of surprise to Plum how much his works were appreciated by academics. No scholar himself, he seemed to have a marked aversion to them. Whenever intellectuals appeared in his books they were usually weedy, timorous young men or overpowering, eccentric women, and were always being mocked and made to look foolish. It must have been with some apprehension, therefore, that in June of 1939 Plum appeared before a large assembly of some of the most notable scholars in Britain. However, he need have had no qualms; he was greeted enthusiastically. It is customary on these occasions for the Public Orator of the University to make a speech in Latin and in this Plum was hailed as 'a magical author', 'a lover of elegant speech', and 'the most pleasant, witty, charming, jocular and humorous of men'. The speech also contained a number of donnish jokes about the rich young man (Bertie Wooster) and his faithful attendant (Jeeves) who was 'a great deviser of stratagems and an arbiter of dress'. Reference was also made to the noble Clarence (Lord Emsworth) and 'his distinguished sow' and to Augustus (Gussie Fink-Nottle), 'the great expert on the love life of newts'.

That evening the University put on a banquet where Plum was one of the guests of honour, and the cry went up for him to make a speech. But it was the old story. Seated alone in front of a typewriter witticisms would have flown freely, but in company he was struck dumb. He could do no more than struggle to his feet, mumble a few words of thanks and then sit down again. He should surely have been prepared to do more than this.

Chapter 12

How true it is that in this world we can never tell behind what corner Fate may not be lurking with the brass knuckles.

Camp was really great fun.

I never met a more cheerful crowd and I loved them like brothers.

On the outbreak of the Second World War several people tried to persuade Plum and Ethel to leave Low Wood, their house in Le Touquet, and come back to England. But for various reasons they stayed put. Low Wood had been their home for four years, longer than any of their other houses, and they had become greatly attached to it. Also returning to England would have meant putting Wonder, the Pekingese, into quarantine, which was unimaginable.

Like most English people at that time the Wodehouses had erroneous ideas about the way the war would go. They were convinced that Germany would soon be starved into surrender and that Allied troops would be marching triumphantly into Berlin. Never did they imagine that the German army would soon be overrunning the whole of France.

With the end of the 'Phoney War' in the spring of 1940 events occurred with bewildering rapidity. The German army seemed unstoppable, but there was still time for Plum and Ethel to get away; but they left it too late and when they did try, their car broke down and they had to come back. The Germans reached Le Touquet soon afterwards and a party of soldiers came to Low Wood and removed all food, tobacco, radios, bicycles and the two cars. Plum was ordered to report to the German command every day, but for the time being there was no other interruption to his normal life, and he continued with his writing. But then an order went out that all Englishmen under sixty were to be interned; Plum was fifty-eight. And so an armed guard escorted him back to Low Wood, and Plum was given ten minutes to pack a suitcase with room for only immediate necessities, but including a few scribbling pads and pencils and one book, chosen on the spur of the moment – the complete works of Shakespeare. He was then taken off to the command post.

During the weeks that followed Plum was shunted around the Continent in conditions of squalor and intense hardship. At first he was taken with other internees to a prison in Loos, where he had to share a small cell with two others – a golf professional and a piano tuner – sleeping on the floor on a straw-filled mattress, and only being let out for half an hour's exercise a day. Later, when they appealed to the German commandant, conditions improved and, to the horror of the French prison guards, the internees were let out of their cells and allowed to roam round the prison. Writing of Loos prison later, Plum's chief memory was 'a good, solid, upstanding smell'.

Fortunately the group was kept only one week at Loos before being transferred by train and cattle trucks to an old army barracks in Liège. Here conditions were a little better, but as soon as they had got the place more or less in order, they were moved on again, this time to a mediaeval mountain fortress at Huy in Belgium. At first sight conditions in Huy seemed appalling. It had been empty for some time and had been left in a filthy state by the Belgian troops who had last occupied it. No preparations had been made for receiving internees, and they were crammed into rooms with no beds, blankets or mattresses. The only bedding available was old army greatcoats and these could not be used safely as they were crawling with lice. Plum was forced to use his raincoat and jacket as blankets and his briefcase and trousers as a pillow. Food of a sort, mainly soup, was provided, but no eating utensils. In order to get one's share it was necessary to scavenge on garbage heaps for an old tin, bottle or can – in Plum's case an old oil can which 'added to the taste of the soup that little something that the others hadn't got'. Everyone was preoccupied with food. All the inmates, especially the young ones, were extremely hungry all the time and constantly on the look-out for any scraps that were going. At meal times everyone kept an eagle eye on everyone else to make sure the food was divided up equally 'to the last millimetre'. And food which before one would never have dreamed of eating – slabs of black bread and lard, crackers hardly distinguishable from dog biscuits and a sort of butter resembling axle grease – became great delicacies and were eagerly sought after. And yet, disgusting and inadequate as the food usually was, Plum could bring himself to write in his Camp Notebook: 'One feels marvellous on it; it is really all one wants.'

Plum was to stay five weeks at Huy, during which time he played his part in the life of the camp – cleaning, fetching, carrying, queuing and endlessly parading. There were two regular parades a day and these should not have lasted long. But they tended to be chaotic and took much longer than necessary. Plum's fellow internees were a polyglot collection – Dutch, Belgians, Bulgarians, Malays and anyone with any connection with England. And they were drawn from all walks of life: priests and professors rubbed shoulders with barmen and bottlewashers, bank managers and golf professionals with tap dancers and merchant seamen. The task of getting this motley crowd into anything like parade ground order was beyond even the German army. They shambled onto parade, hands in pockets, making some effort to stand to attention, but then moving off to have a chat with a friend. The German sergeants and corporals tried to smarten things up, but could not as there was the language problem; all orders had to be given through interpreters and this took a long time and in any case nobody seemed to take much notice. One of the main irritants at Huy was the frequent calling of extra parades, usually for some trivial announcement such as that everyone must shave every day or that internees were not to hang around the cookhouse. On one occasion an extra parade was called for the solemn proclamation that stealing was prohibited.

Fussy and fierce as the German guards sometimes were, it seems that generally they treated the inmates well. Plum's Camp Notebook contained many references to individual acts of kindness, such as giving away their own food and cigarettes, buying things at local shops and helping to make living conditions more tolerable. Some of the guards had read Plum's books, and he was particularly touched when one of them came up to him and said: 'Thank you for Jeeves.' Plum wrote in his Camp Notebook: 'I never met an English-speaking German I did not like instantly.' But this sympathetic feeling was dangerous; it estranged Plum more and more from the war and could have been partly responsible for the tragic error of judgement he was to make in the following year.

In September 1940, after another horrendous journey of three days and three nights crammed into railway carriages with virtually no food or water, Plum and his fellow internees were moved to another camp, this time a disused lunatic asylum in Tost in eastern Germany. Grisly as this sounded, it was in fact a great improvement on anywhere they had been before. Plum was delighted to see on arrival that it was a going concern with other internees already there. It was not, as previously, a squalid semi-derelict building which had to be cleansed throughout and adapted for use. Also there was far more space. 'If you had a cat,' Plum wrote, 'and had wished to swing it, you could have done so quite easily in our new surroundings.' There were other advantages as well: food parcels began to arrive regularly, so too did letters, although for security reasons these had to be torn up as soon as they had been read. Plum's greatest worry had been what had happened to Ethel, and now he was reassured that she was safe and well. Another benefit for Plum at Tost was that he was excused heavy duties. He could not help being rather smug about this:

> *When there was man's work to be done, like hauling coal or shovelling snow, we just sat and looked on, swapping reminiscences of the Victorian age, while our juniors snapped into it. I don't know anything that so braces one up on a cold winter morning, with an Upper Silesian blizzard doing its stuff, as to light one's pipe and look out of the window and watch a gang of younger men shovelling snow. It makes you realize what the man meant who said that Age has its pleasures as well as Youth.*

There were certain fatigues which were eagerly sought after, like acting as a server or carrier of meals and working in the cookhouse; for these involved double rations. But for ordinary fatigues, like hauling coal, the only reward was the joy of labour:

> *I suppose a really altruistic young man would have been all pepped by the thought, after he had put in an hour or two of hauling coal, that he had been promoting the happiness of the greatest number, but I never heard one of our toilers talk along these lines. It was more usual to hear them say that, next time their turn came along, they were ruddy well going to sprain an ankle and report sick.*

But what Plum appreciated most at Tost was that internees were given more time and freedom to do what they wanted. For some this meant games or getting up plays and concerts. Classes too were available in such subjects as first aid, languages and shorthand. But for Plum, of course, it was writing. In the horrors of the previous months – crammed into filthy prison cells, packed into overcrowded trains or cattle trucks, always hungry and dirty and in too close contact with variegated humanity – he had always known that he must keep writing. It was the breath of life to him. He had paper and pencils with him and even in the grimmest conditions he had been able to scribble down ideas for a new book. In Tost conditions were easier, but still often chaotic: there were usually games going on all around him and sometimes there would be 'two Germans standing behind me with rifles, breathing down the back of my neck'. Later Plum wrote to his friend, William Townend:

> *I'm so glad you enjoyed* Money in the Bank. *The only novel, I should imagine, that has ever been written in an internment camp. I did it at the rate of about a page a day in a room with over fifty men playing cards and ping-pong and talking and singing. The first twelve chapters were written in a whirl of ping-pong balls. I suppose on an average morning I would get from fifteen to twenty on the side of the head just as I was searching for the* mot juste.

Later he was allowed privileges: a room was allotted to him (actually a padded cell) where he could do his work, but he did not always have exclusive use of this, sometimes finding himself sharing it with such people as a saxophonist getting in a little practice or a tap-dancer

Plum in internment: always writing

warming up, or someone having a viva voce rehearsal of a lecture he was about to give. But Plum's extraordinary powers of concentration overcame these distractions, *Money in the Bank* is surely one of his best books.

Plum was to stay at Tost for nearly a year, and so adaptable was he that at the end of that time he could write in all sincerity: 'Camp was really great fun.' Perhaps one reason for his enjoyment of it was that it reminded him of his school-days – Plum's golden age. Once again he was leading a community life, sharing experiences with others, being bossed about – often tiresomely but not brutally – and trying not to be caught in minor offences like smoking in the corridors. And after twenty years he played cricket, or a sort of cricket, again. Even the German guards would join in this, retrieving balls which had been hit through the barbed wire fence with their bayonets. And, just as at school it was a red-letter day when a 'hamper' with jam and sweets and other goodies arrived from home, so also it was at the camp when Red Cross parcels arrived with such things as chocolate, tobacco, condensed milk and warm clothing. In view of his age and distinction Plum was offered a bedroom of his own at Tost, but this he refused, preferring to remain in a dormitory with more than sixty others enjoying its camaraderie and good humour. A mixed bag though his companions might be, he became very fond of them and enjoyed their company.

Chapter 13

I ought to have had the sense to see that it was a loony thing to do.

You can never trust a writer not to make an ass of himself.

1941 was to be a fateful year for P. G. Wodehouse. His life became blighted and he never recovered from it.

In 1940 life had been looking up for him. The camp commandant had been sympathetic, offering him a room to himself, providing him with a typewriter and seeing to it that the script of his recently finished novel, *Money in the Bank*, was sent to his agent in New York, America not yet having come into the war. All seemed to be going well, but at the end of the year his troubles began when an American journalist sought permission for an interview with him, which was granted provided that it was attended by a Gestapo officer to vet what was said. This proved unnecessary as the questions and answers were light-hearted and innocuous. However, the tone of what Plum said, putting on a brave face and depicting internment as something of a joke, was taken amiss in England as showing Germans in a favourable light. When it was published at the very end of 1940 it had ominous repercussions. It awoke the German Foreign Office to the significance of Plum. Perhaps he might like to make a broadcast to America about life in an internment camp. At the time the Germans were doing all they could to keep America out of the war and a broadcast by a world-renowned author showing humane and kindly treatment being meted out to internees would have propaganda value. And so the camp commandant was told to throw a fly over Plum about such an idea; and Plum reacted positively. He saw in it an opportunity to thank his American well-wishers who had written to him and sent him food parcels; it would also keep him in touch with his readers in America and keep his books in the public eye. Surely, he thought, there could be no harm in that. But, as was to be seen, there was terrible harm in it.

When it became known that Plum was interested in broadcasting, the German Foreign Office did all it could to promote the idea and so to enmesh him that he could not get out of it. It was allowed that an article he had written on camp life, *My War with Germany*, be sent to America, where it was published in the *Saturday Evening Post*. More importantly, the Gestapo was persuaded to agree to his early release from internment. On 21st June 1941 (the day Germany invaded Russia) Plum was summoned to the office of the camp commandant and told to pack his things and be ready to go. At the time he was still four months off his sixtieth birthday, when he would have been due for release in the normal course of events. He was then sent with two guards to Berlin, where they looked for suitable hotel accommodation, but Berlin was full at the time and all that could be found was a suite in a luxury hotel, the Adlon, which Plum took (at his own expense), little knowing what embarrassment and ill will it was to cause him later. An old friend from Hollywood days came to see him – a Baron von Barnekow, an Americanised German, believed by Plum to be strongly anti-Nazi. The Baron could not have been more helpful, providing Plum with much needed money and clothing. There also came to Plum another German he had known slightly in Hollywood, Werner Plack, now an agent of the German Foreign Office; and it was he who pursued the subject of broadcasts to America. He suggested that Plum should make a series of five, in which he would be given freedom to say what he liked with no censorship; and to this Plum agreed, a decision he was bitterly to regret.

The timing of this agreement is important as it was later to be alleged that, by means of it, Plum secured his early release from internment, but this was not the case. If Plum had been more politically minded he would not have fallen into this trap. But he should have known better. He entirely failed to realise that any broadcast from Germany in time of war, however harmless and humorous, would be taken as an endorsement of the Nazi regime. Later in life, admitting he had made a terrible mistake, he pleaded in mitigation that a year in an internment camp had sapped his intellect. Since the fall of France he had heard nothing of the war except what the Germans had chosen to tell him; if he had been more aware he might have realised the tremendous importance in modern warfare of propaganda.

Like his magazine articles Plum's broadcasts contained

nothing political nor treasonable. Basically they were cheerful, chatty accounts of life in an internment camp entitled 'How to be an Internee and Like it'. But coming at that particular time, when Britain's fortunes were at their lowest and the country was in mortal danger, the fact that they were made at all caused an uproar. The situation was made worse by the way in which news of the broadcasts broke in Britain. At the same time it was made known that Plum had been released early from internment and was living in a luxury suite in the Adlon Hotel. This was explosive stuff. In time of war the least sign of treachery induces frenzy. The immediate reaction was that Plum had made a deal with the Germans – that in return for being released early and lodged in luxury he would broadcast on German radio, and it was assumed that in those circumstances the broadcasts would be pro-German. But, as has been seen, this was not the case. No deal had been made and no pressure put on Plum as to what he should say.

In the weeks after his release Plum's troubles deepened all the time. He seemed incapable of putting a foot right. Just before his first broadcast he gave an interview to the correspondent of Columbia Broadcasting; this contained nothing inflammatory but showed indifference to the war and an aloofness as to its outcome. He seemed more interested in the fate of his books: '. . . something that has been bothering me a good deal. I'm wondering whether the kind of people and the kind of England I write about will live after the war whether England wins or not, I mean.' A damning statement, all too easily misinterpreted. Two days later, on 28th June, a recording

125

of his first talk was broadcast and then the fat was well and truly in the fire. Being transmitted only to America and in the middle of the night it was heard by very few people in Britain, but this did not prevent an outburst of furious indignation. A question was asked in parliament and the foreign secretary, Anthony Eden, replied tersely that His Majesty's government had seen with regret that Mr Wodehouse had lent his services to the German propaganda machine. Outraged people wrote to the newspapers expressing dismay and horror. These included a number of Plum's fellow authors. His old friend, Ian Hay, with whom he had collaborated on plays and musicals, wrote more in sorrow than in anger that Plum could have no realisation what he was doing. He urged that 'immediate steps be taken to inform our much beloved but misguided Plum to lay off. He must be made to know that no broadcast from Berlin by a world-famous Englishman, however "neutral" in tone, can serve as anything but an advertisement for Hitler, and that no word of his can help our cause, and hardly any word can fail to help the enemy.' These were wise and generous words, but other people were less temperate.

A. A. Milne, another old friend, took time off from writing about Christopher Robin to write a letter to *The Times* in which he accused Plum of always avoiding his responsibilities. He had, he said, escaped into a dream world of his own and wanted no part of the unpleasant and inconvenient things of life. He also referred, rather obscurely, to Plum as a licensed humorist whose licence would now be withdrawn. With more justification, if somewhat sententiously, Milne then urged Plum to realise that 'though a genius may grant himself an enviable position above the battle where civic and social responsibilities are concerned, there are times when every man has to come down into the arena, pledge himself to the cause in which he believes and suffer for it'.

Others to join in the fray included the distinguished writer, Dorothy Sayers, who stressed how difficult it must have been for Plum to realise what he was doing when he had been isolated from the war for so long: 'Theoretically, no doubt, every patriotic person should be prepared to resist enemy pressure to the point of martyrdom; but it must be far more difficult to bear such heroic witness when its urgent necessity is not, and cannot be, understood.' Another writer, Ethel Mannin, urged that judgement on Plum should be withheld until the facts were known, and to Plum's detractors she cautioned: 'Judge not that ye be not judged.'

Another correspondent took a different line. Sean O'Casey, the Irish writer, said that Plum was such an insignificant figure in English humorous literature, or any literature at all, that it was to the advantage of England that he should broadcast for the Germans. 'If England,' he wrote, 'has any dignity left in the way of literature, she will forget forever the antics of English Literature's performing flea.' In later years Plum was to seize on this phrase: 'Thinking it over I believe he meant to be complimentary, for all the performing fleas I have met have impressed me with their sterling artistry and that indefinable something which makes the good trouper.' Subsequently he named one of his volumes of autobiography *Performing Flea*.

Plum's friends had done their best for him and his critics had had their say, and it might have been that the storm would have died down. There was a disposition to think that he was 'more fool than knave', and was behaving like Bertie Wooster without the guidance of Jeeves. But unfortunately the affair was stirred up when an article Plum had written while in internment (*My War with Germany*) appeared in the *Saturday Evening Post*. Like the broadcasts it contained nothing political or disloyal, but it showed how offhand was Plum's attitude to the war. Tost was described as 'a home from home which, if he were a bachelor without dogs, he would be in no hurry to leave'. And there was a frivolous suggestion about a separate peace between himself and the Germans:

> *It should be simple to arrive at some settlement which would be satisfactory to both parties. The only concession I want from Germany is that she give me a loaf of bread, tell the gentlemen with the muskets at the main gate to look the other way and leave the rest to me.*
>
> *In return for this I am prepared to hand over India and an autographed set of my books and to reveal a secret process for cooking sliced potatoes on the radiator known only to internee Grant and myself. This firm offer holds good till Wednesday week.*

Once again inept and foolish rather than treasonable, but it gave support to the contention of Plum's critics that he was distancing himself from the war and wanted to have nothing to do with it.

At another time there might not have been such an

outcry and people would have waited until all the facts were known before passing judgement. But in 1941 Britain's situation was desperate. Hitler's armies had been everywhere victorious. The only hope of an Allied victory lay in America coming into the war; and for this the propaganda campaign was vital. The Americans had to be convinced of the wickedness of the German people and the absolute necessity of defeating them. And in this Plum's efforts, showing a humane and inoffensive side of the German character, were not helpful; it was thought by some to have had a small but significant adverse effect. It was decided, therefore, that a counter-blast was necessary and that Plum's name should be blackened. In this the lead was taken by the minister of the crown responsible for propaganda, the Right Hon. Alfred Duff Cooper (later Lord Norwich), a brilliant, if somewhat erratic, politician and a writer of distinction. His chosen instrument for the task was a *Daily Mirror* columnist, William Connor, known as Cassandra, a specialist in bitter and vituperative journalism. Connor approached his task with relish; it was the sort of thing he could do supremely well. Abuse, rhetoric and righteous indignation – it was on these that he would rely; truth would be secondary.

In his character assassination of Plum, Connor scraped up every evil morsel he could imagine. He alleged that Plum had spent the First World War making money in New York. This had some truth, but it omitted the vital point that Plum had, through poor eyesight, failed the medical test for the services. Connor further asserted that Plum had defrauded the income tax authorities. This also was untrue, as was the ridiculous further allegation he made that Plum had made a pact with his country's enemies and 'fallen on his knees and worshipped Hitler'. All the worst atrocities of the war were associated with his name; in particular the bombing of London was graphically described and the plight of the victims contrasted with Plum, supposedly basking in luxury in the Adlon Hotel. Some of the accusations were patently absurd: because Plum lived in Le Touquet he must spend his life gambling; because he had written about idle playboys, he must be one himself. Plum's life, most of which had been spent toiling away at his typewriter, was described as 'forty years of money-making fun'. Even the ludicrously fabricated story of Plum throwing a cocktail party at Le Touquet when the Germans arrived was resurrected.

When the B.B.C. governors saw the script of this malignant diatribe they were horrified. They thought it libellous and in 'execrable taste', and forbade it to be broadcast. But in wartime the Minister of Information had the power to overrule them, and this he proceeded to do: the broadcast was made not only to America but also at peak listening time on the Home Service in Britain. The result was, as some at the B.B.C. had predicted, that there was a wave of sympathy in favour of Plum. The broadcast was so abusive and unfair that in some quarters it had the opposite effect to the one intended. Newspapers were beset with angry letters complaining of this 'cheap, slanderous, feeble-violent talk'. In reply the Minister wrote to *The Times* to say that, although some people might find the broadcast in bad taste, occasions might arise in time of war when plain speaking was more desirable than good taste. Connor too replied in typical vein: 'I have been condemned on the grounds of bad taste. Since when has it been bad taste to name and nail a traitor to England? The letters you have published have only served as a sad demonstration that there is still in this country a section of the community eager and willing to defend its own quislings [traitors]'. Connor claimed that over ninety per cent of the letters received by the *Daily Mirror* had approved of what he had said and that they came from a representative slice of the community which outnumbered *The Times* readership by ten to one – 'the vast masses of whom were fighting men, factory workers, miners and the ordinary common people who are carrying the burden of this war'.

Remarkably Plum was not to bear Connor any malice for what he said. He always found it difficult to hate anybody, and perhaps he sensed that Connor was just doing a 'hatchet' job without any real bitterness. Years later, when Plum was living in America, he had lunch with Connor and they took a liking to each other, and carried on a friendly correspondence until Connor died.

Plum proceeded to deliver the five broadcasts agreed. As before, there was nothing in them that was political or treasonable. For the most part they were jocular and frivolous, at times in language that might have been used by Bertie Wooster. At the same time they confirmed the impression given before that he was unconcerned with the war and wanted to have nothing to do with it. 'I am quite unable,' he wrote, 'to work up any kind of belligerent feeling. Just as I'm about to feel belligerent about some country I meet a decent sort of chap. We go out together and lose any fighting thoughts or feelings.' Remarks such as these could be misconstrued and used against him by his enemies.

Before the broadcasts had been completed a new note of bitterness was introduced. At first they had been orchestrated by the German Foreign Office, which sought to present Plum as a distinguished British citizen innocently caught up in the war, patriotic and fair minded and with no sympathy for Nazism and whose commendation of German humane ways would therefore carry great weight, particularly in America, to whom the talks would be solely directed. But when it became evident how great was the furore caused by the talks, Goebbels, the propaganda chief (between whom and the Foreign Office there was a deadly feud), decided that the talks would be more damaging if Plum was presented as a Nazi sympathiser and his talks relayed to Britain as well as to America. And he had his way.

But there were to be no more broadcasts nor humorous magazine articles. For it became clear to Plum how much harm they had done his reputation both in England and America, where the editor of the *Saturday Evening Post* (despite having just serialised *My War with Germany*) informed Plum he would stop publishing his works unless he gave a guarantee that he would not broadcast again; and Plum complied.

Plum paid dearly for his lack of judgement. The stain of it never left him. That it was a great folly no one can deny, least of all Plum himself, who was always to refer to it as 'a loony thing to have done'. The only excuse he made was that for a year he had been shut up, away from the world and in ignorance of what was going on. This has some validity but, politically green as he undoubtedly was, he should have had some idea of the horrors of Nazism and the fearful danger threatening his country; and that his attitude, which seemed to be one of near neutrality, would arouse strong feelings. Basically he was incapable of dealing with the situation that confronted him – suddenly released from the rigours of an internment camp, ushered into a luxury Berlin hotel and then beset with friendly and accommodating acquaintances, he was all too vulnerable and ready to swim with the tide. His qualities of humility, gentleness and gratitude left him open to the wiles of scheming intelligence officers.

To understand fully how he succumbed one has to be aware, as George Orwell pointed out at the time, that for a dedicated author writing was the essence of his being, and Plum was afraid that, because of the war and his own disappearance from the scene, his books would become neglected and he himself forgotten. He had therefore, he felt, to take any opportunity to bring himself to the notice of the reading public. That he should have made the mistake of thinking that this consideration outweighed all others was due to a blind spot in his make-up. Most men of genius have these and do not think straight on some subjects. And so it was with Plum and politics.

It must be the case that he was unaware that he was doing anything harmful or treasonable; he could not see that light-hearted, non-political chit-chat to neutral America could be damaging.

How much damage in fact the broadcasts did is open to question; it could be maintained with the wisdom of hindsight that it was negligible. If the purpose of the Germans in promoting them was to keep America neutral they clearly failed. Six months later, following the Japanese attack on Pearl Harbour, America was at war with Germany.

Chapter 14

The voice of calumny is never silent.

I am enjoying life amazingly these days. Thunderclouds fill the sky in every direction, but I continue to be happy.

A week after his release from Tost, Plum was moved from Berlin to a house in the small village of Degenershaus in the Harz mountains. There he was treated as an honoured guest by Baroness von Bodenhausen, a cousin of von Barnekow, an Anglophile and anti-Nazi. For Plum this was a perfect resting place – remote from the war, a tranquil farming community where he received every kindness and was left to himself when he wanted to get on with his writing. He had then three books on the stocks – *Money in the Bank*, *Full Moon*, and was planning the plot of another, *Spring Fever*.

A month later he was joined by Ethel, along with Wonder the peke. During the last year Ethel had been on the move. Soon after Plum had been interned Low Wood was commandeered by the Germans and it had been necessary for her, with peke and parrot, to move into a furnished room on a trout farm. But this had not been to her liking and she moved soon afterwards to a bed-sitting room in Lille. Here too she became restless and moved into a house in the country, where she stayed as a paying guest until she was brought to Berlin.

Plum was to spend two years in Germany, sometimes in the Harz mountains, sometimes in Berlin (unfortunately at the Adlon Hotel) and sometimes as a paying guest on an estate in Silesia. During this time the fortunes of war changed dramatically. The Germans, who hitherto had been all-victorious, were now on the defensive. They suffered heavy defeats at Stalingrad and in North Africa, America had come into the war against them, and Allied bombing raids were increasing in intensity. Berlin was under heavy bombardment, and in September 1943 Plum was given permission to move to Paris, where he stayed until the liberation of the city nearly a year later. During this time money was a pressing problem. It was, of course, impossible to draw on Plum's funds in England or America, and so Plum and Ethel had to scrape together what they could in France. They borrowed some, Ethel sold her jewellery, and some money was forthcoming from a Spanish publisher for royalties on Wodehouse books sold in Spain. Plum also obtained a sum of money from a German film company for the film rights on one of his books – arguably a technical offence for a British citizen, as it contravened a wartime regulation banning all trade with the enemy.

When the Allies entered Paris in August 1944 Plum was living reasonably comfortably in the Bristol Hotel. It was not likely that he would be left in peace for long. The British would be wanting to take up with him the matter of his broadcasts and his relations generally with the Germans during the war. It was a piece of great good fortune for Plum that the first British agent sent to interview him was the well-known author and journalist (and later broadcaster), Malcolm Muggeridge. A man of sardonic humour and strong, unorthodox views, he was an unusual intelligence officer. Later he described this visit:

> *I had made no sort of preparation for my visit, and had no plan as to how I should approach Wodehouse. It was difficult to know where to begin. I attempted the banal observation that his books had given me great pleasure. Even this was not strictly true. With my strict socialist childhood, Bertie Wooster and Jeeves had about them a flavour of forbidden fruit; like Sade or Casanova in the eyes of a Methodist. To me Wodehouse was just a distinguished and highly original writer, and, as such, entitled to be kept clear of the atrocious buffooneries of power maniacs and their wars. Otherwise, I had no feeling about the matter at all.[1]*

It might have been expected that in this, his first encounter with British authority, Plum would have been grilled relentlessly about his wartime activities, but instead he and Muggeridge had a long, amiable chat about mutual acquaintances and the literary scene in England:

> *As we went on talking the evening shadows began to fill the room. There was no electricity and so no possibility of turning on a light. I have always loved sitting in a darkening room and talking. It takes the sharp edge off the exigencies of time. In Paris on that particular evening the moment was*

---

[1] From *Tread Softly for you Tread on my Jokes* by Malcolm Muggeridge (Collins, 1966).

particularly exquisite, if only because of the contrast between the tranquillity where we were and the mounting confusion and shooting outside. I was happy to be spending it with Wodehouse. He sent down for a bottle of wine, which we consumed as we talked.[2]

In the weeks that followed not all Plum's interviews with authority were to be as agreeable as this, but Muggeridge was always at hand to help him and give him what protection he could. For Paris after the liberation was a dangerous city. The citizens were in a vicious and ugly mood. Everyone was accusing everyone else of having collaborated with the Germans. Men were being beaten up and summarily put to death, and women were being lynched and having their heads shaved. Of course the people who took the lead in this mob rule had been, as often as not, collaborators themselves and were now seeking to expiate their sins by taking it out on others – what George Orwell called 'the punishment of the guilty by the guilty'. In this atmosphere Plum, with the shadow of the broadcasts hanging over him, was particularly vulnerable. He was perhaps fortunate that nothing worse happened to him than that he was arrested by the French police. This came out of the blue and seems to have originated with a chance remark by an English woman at a dinner party that it was a scandal that such notorious traitors as the Wodehouses should be at large in Paris. Whereupon a prefect of police, who was also at the party, immediately gave orders that they should be arrested.

[2] Op. cit.

And so, in the watches of the night, leather-clad figures brandishing machine guns arrived at the Bristol Hotel and took Plum, along with Ethel and Wonder, off to the Palais de Justice. Here nobody knew why they were there or what was to be done with them, and for nearly a day they were kept waiting in a corridor while Ethel and Wonder fretted and Plum, with his usual disregard for his surroundings, got quietly on with his next book (*Uncle Dynamite*). However, their guardian angel in the form of Malcolm Muggeridge was soon on the scene with a supply of corned beef, cigars and champagne. He has given a hilarious description of what happened next:

> *No one seemed to know why M. and Mme, Wodenhorse (as they appeared on the warrant) were there, and I had no difficulty in arranging for Ethel's immediate release. As far as I could gather, in her highly individual French she had reduced the whole Sûreté to a condition of prostration and panic. Also, she had her peke, Wonder, with her, and, by the time I arrived on the scene, the police were desperately anxious to get both Ethel and Wonder off the premises. More difficult was to get permission for Wodehouse to have his razor returned to him. This involved filling in an enormous form, whose items I only imperfectly understood. I went out and got some food and we all lunched together. What with everyone else accusing everyone else of collaboration, and the Palais de Justice itself being in a state of total confusion, the administration of justice, as may be imagined, proceeded even more lamely and imprecisely than usual.*
>
> *It appeared that the only way to ameliorate Wodehouse's lot was for him to be ill. This presented difficulties. His*

equanimity had not been disturbed by his arrest, and he looked pink and well. However, an amiable prison doctor felt his pulse, shook his head, and decided that he should be transferred to a clinic. The only one available was a maternity home, and there Wodehouse stayed for some weeks, with ladies having babies all round him. Each day the doctor took his temperature, which was normal. Two guards were posted at his door. He used to play cards with them in the evenings. His mornings were spent, as always, in writing.[3]

For some time to come, however, Plum's situation was to be precarious; it was touch and go whether he would be prosecuted for treason. Already before his arrest he had been closely interrogated by a Major Cussen, who was in charge of the investigation of 'renegades'. This had lasted ten days, and at the end of it Cussen told Muggeridge: 'Wodehouse must be exonerated of everything but foolishness and one or two minor technical offences.' And the Director of Public Prosecutions in London, after reading Cussen's report, gave it as his opinion that 'on the present material there is not sufficient evidence to justify a prosecution of this man'. He added, however, that further evidence in Germany might come to light which could alter the situation. Both Cussen and Muggeridge agreed that Plum should be kept out of England for the present. If he were to come within the jurisdiction of the English courts he might be put on trial. Already questions were being asked in parliament as to why this had not happened. Another threat to Plum

[3] Op cit

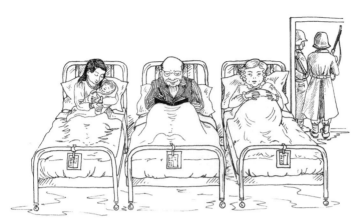

Plum under arrest in a maternity ward

might have come from the new British ambassador to France – Alfred Duff Cooper, his persecutor at the time of the broadcasts. But in the event he showed no inclination to press matters further.

For some time Plum continued to be beset with worries and misfortunes. In England there were still demands for his prosecution 'for treasonable acts committed during the recent war', and the government was taking the line that 'the matter would be reconsidered if and when Mr Wodehouse comes within the jurisdiction of our courts' – a clear warning to him to keep out of the country. In America too there was some strong feeling against him. At first publishers were cautious about handling his work, and the Inland Revenue Service in America chose this moment to continue to pursue Plum in relation to the question of the amount of American tax which should have been paid in the 1930s by someone who had already paid tax on the same income in another country. In the event this claim was proved unjustifiable and the matter was settled largely in Plum's favour, but it meant that for the time being his money in America was frozen when he needed it most, and life in Paris during the years immediately after the war was not comfortable. Food and fuel were in very short supply, and Plum had to spend long hours queuing and fetching and carrying. And yet, as always, he remained cheerful. 'Thunderclouds fill the sky,' he wrote to a friend, 'but I continue to be happy.'

Another trouble at this time was that his writing was going through a difficult phase. By the end of the war he had four completed novels in stock. These were published over the next two or three years both in the UK and in the USA, and in the UK his sales soon went to pre-war levels. However, he went through a sort of writer's block and found it difficult to get back into his old writing routine. Also he was feeling the onset of old age: 'I find increasing age has slowed me up a lot. I can no longer do what I used to consider a decent day's work. I have to force it out in drops, relying on technique instead of exuberance.' And in the egalitarian post-war world would anybody be interested in his kind of writing? To a friend he wrote: 'What the devil does one write about these days if one is a specialist on country houses and butlers, both of which have ceased to exist?' During the war years the sale of his books had declined, and in the mood of the moment some public libraries had taken it upon themselves to ban his books. But from 1945 the situation began to change. In the bleak and colourless years of post-war Britain people were finding in the golden world of Wodehouse a blissful escape. Despite

During his stay in Paris, Plum seldom missed out on his daily
dozen, sometimes in the Bois de Boulogne with Wonder

continued attacks from journalists and politicians sales of his works began to rise, and when *Money in the Bank*, the novel he had written in internment, was published in 1946, it was received with great delight. At the time butlers might be few and far between and country houses falling down, but they had not lost their magic.

After living in temporary accommodation for so long it had become imperative for the Wodehouses to come to a decision about a permanent home. They considered going back to Low Wood in Le Touquet, but it had been badly damaged during the war and they had no immediate funds for rebuilding it. For the present England seemed barred to them, and in any case the main reason for their settling there had been removed. In the last weeks of the war their beloved daughter, Leonora, had died after an operation. Of all the blows he had received lately this, for Plum, was the hardest. 'I thought she was immortal,' he said when Malcolm Muggeridge broke the news to him. More and more, therefore, the Wodehouses were turning their thoughts towards America. For many years America had been a second home to Plum, and there was, he was assured, plenty of work for him there, especially in the theatre. And, compared with Europe, America at that time was a land of plenty – there were no queues there for a loaf of bread and a few pounds of potatoes. The difficulty was to obtain a passage. At that time it would have to be by sea, and all ships crossing the Atlantic were fully booked for months ahead. But this did seem their best hope, and so passages were booked and in time became available, and in April 1947 Plum, Ethel and the apparently immortal Wonder set off to New York.

Chapter 15

Every time I come back to New York it's like meeting an old sweetheart and finding she has put on a lot of weight.

To be a humorist one must see the world out of focus. You must, in other words, be slightly cock-eyed.

Plum was given a friendly welcome when he arrived in New York. Feeling against him had never been as strong in America as in England, and the pressmen, who swarmed aboard his ship, did not grill him aggressively about his wartime activities. Soon after landing he gave a broadcast which was picked up by 350 radio stations.

The Wodehouses settled comfortably into New York. Money was supposed to be in short supply, but this did not prevent them from putting up at the Savoy Plaza Hotel until they found themselves an apartment in one of the more expensive parts of the city. Their financial situation was relieved when Plum's publisher decided the time had come that he could publish safely the five books he had written since the outbreak of war; and these were well received. But Plum had difficulty in finding work in the theatre; he soon discovered a very different scene here from the one he had known before the war. He wrote to his old collaborator, Guy Bolton:

> *I can't get used to the new Broadway. Apparently you have to write your show and get it composed and then give a series of auditions to backers, instead of having the management line up a couple of stars and then get a show written for them. It's so damn difficult to write a show without knowing who you are writing it for. It's like trying to write lyrics without a book. I feel lost without you.*

Plum also discovered that there was no longer a sure market for his work in American magazines. Here too the scene had changed. Many had disappeared because of shortage of paper, and the demand was for shorter stories with an American flavour, so that Wodehouse, once in great demand, found himself an outsider. For the first time since his early youth he was receiving rejection slips.

In the following year Ethel paid a visit to England. Plum did not accompany her as it was still considered unsafe for him to come within the jurisdiction of British courts. One of the objects of her visit was to persuade the Bank of England to 'unfreeze' the sum of money which had built up from the sales of Wodehouse books since 1939. However, the only concession she could obtain was that the Bank of England would pay from these funds the cost of her stay at the Ritz Hotel. In order to obtain spending money she had to borrow from the hall porter who then put the amount borrowed on the hotel bill. Characteristically, Ethel then went off to

France to try to find the parrot she had had before the war and from which she had been parted in the course of her travels. History does not relate if she was successful.

In the following year Plum was granted an immigrant's visa into America. This was important for two reasons. In the first place it gave the Wodehouses stability; they could now make America their permanent home. In a letter at the time Plum wrote:

> *Unless I plot to upset the American government by violence – which I doubt if I shall do; you know how busy one is – I can't be taken by the seat of the trousers and slung out.*

Being a resident in America also meant that Plum's money in England could be released; from then on the Wodehouses never again had financial worries. In the same year they moved into a plush penthouse in Park Avenue ('so convenient for walking Wonder in Central Park'), but they were not destined to stay there long. Three years later, when they were visiting Guy Bolton at Remsenburg in Long Island, Ethel suddenly took it into her head to buy a house there. At first it was not intended that they should live in it permanently, only for the summer months. Plum wrote at the time: 'The whole point of our buying this house was that we could have a place where we could turn the key and go away whenever we wanted to.' In the event they found themselves spending more and more time there, so that they sold the New York apartment and, far from going away whenever they wanted, hardly ever emerged from Remsenburg for the rest of their lives.

The house at Remsenburg was of no great beauty, but it was attractively situated in twelve acres of land leading down to a creek. It was not likely that Ethel would be satisfied with it as it stood, and she lost no time in putting in hand plans for redevelopment. The gardens and woodlands were replanted and the house enlarged and embellished. As always Plum gave her her head but took a somewhat wry attitude to her activities. In a letter at the time he wrote:

> *Ethel has been buying trees like a drunken sailor – if drunken sailors do buy trees – and though we shall have to go on the dole very soon the result is rather wonderful.*

And in another letter:

> *The house really is fine now. Ethel's new sun parlour is terrific. Huge windows on every side and a great view of the estate. This morning they are putting in the bar in a small room on the other side of the house. God knows why we want a bar, but Ethel thought it a good idea. What is supposed to happen is that the County saunter in for a drink, and we mix it at the bar. The County little knows that if they come within a mile of us we shall take to the hills. But that's Ethel. She really loves solitude as much as you and I do, but she has occasional yearnings to be the Society hostess and go in for all that 'Act 2, The terrace at Meadowsweet Manor' stuff.*

148

In Long Island Plum soon settled into a deep and comfortable rut from which he had little wish ever to emerge: Swedish exercises before breakfast; the morning at his typewriter; in the afternoon a walk with the dogs to the post office to pick up his mail; in the evening a cocktail or two and then reading. Not an exciting routine, but for Plum a completely satisfying one. Malcolm Muggeridge, who had become a great family friend, visited them on several occasions. In 1957, when Plum was seventy-six, he found him 'just the same – a little older, a bit distrait, but in good order'. They went on long walks together and talked on all manner of subjects including 'writers, income tax, the torture of pleasure and the pleasure of work'. Ethel too had changed little:

> *Ethel moves restlessly all the while about the house, heavily made up, crouching forward. Somehow I love her dearly – something tough and wonderful about her. More real, more admirable, than P.G., who's also dear, but occasionally so strangely like their old dog Bill – waiting for his food, padding about in the garden.*[1]

But Muggeridge came to realise that with Plum there were certain barriers that could not be penetrated; this was especially the case with the Berlin broadcasts and the treatment that had been meted out to him because of them; this was a subject from which he always shied away:

---

[1] From *Like It Was*, Malcolm Muggeridge (Collins)

As with all imaginative people there is an area of inner reserve in Wodehouse which one never penetrates. The scars of his time in the stocks are hidden there. In one of his rare references to the experience he said to me that it had made him feel like a music hall comedian, accustomed to applause, who suddenly gets the bird. This, I think, is what it signified to him, and, perhaps, indeed, what it signifies.[2]

It was unthinkable, of course, that Plum should ever give up writing. Death, when it came, would surely find him with a book on the stocks and probably seated in front of his typewriter. He had been greatly concerned that in the post-war world, with its taste for stark, salacious literature, there would be no demand for his kind of writing. But such was not the case. People continued to read his works, and not only the English-speaking world; they were translated into numerous foreign languages. This must surely have caused problems. How, for example, were some of Bertie Wooster's fruitier utterances to be construed into Japanese or, for that matter, any other language? How could be rendered such expressions as 'Bung ho', 'all boomps-a-daisy', or 'putting on the old nosebag', or the American slang of such characters as Soup Slattery and Dolly Molloy – 'oompus-boompus', 'a hunk of baloney' or 'a two-timing piece of cheese'. In *The Penguin Wodehouse Companion* Richard Usborne has a most amusing chapter on French translations of Wodehouse idioms. Four of these might be quoted:

[2] Op cit.

Loony to the eyebrows	*Complètement dingo*
His eyes popped out of his head and waved about on their stalks.	*Ses yeux étaient hors de la tête et erraient de-ci, de-là au bout de leur tige, le nerf optique sans doute.*
To spot oompus-boompus	*Mettre le doigt sur less manigances*
Love's young dream had stubbed its toe	*Le rêve jeunesse et d'amour avait les ailes coupées.*

Like other great English writers who were read extensively abroad, notably Charles Dickens, Plum was responsible for creating a false impression of England among foreigners. So vivid was his writing that many came to believe that his characters were true to life, and that England really was peopled by the likes of Bertie Wooster, Gussie Fink-Nottle and Boko Fittleworth. One bizarre instance of this, recorded by Malcolm Muggeridge, occurred during the Second World War when the Germans dropped a spy into England, dressed, as they imagined to be the fashion, like a member of the Drones Club, complete with monocle and spats. He was, of course, immediately arrested, which was a pity, because if he had made his way to London and gone into a smart restaurant, he might, in the manner of Drones Club members, have started throwing rolls at fellow diners or tossing soft-boiled eggs into electric fans.

During the twenty-one years he lived at Remsenburg Plum wrote twenty-two books as well as numerous letters, including handwritten replies to all fan mail. Wisely he did not attempt a new style of novel; he stayed with the ones he could do best. Of the thirty books five were set at Blandings and seven concerned Jeeves and Bertie Wooster, and many other old friends – Uncle Fred, Lord Uffenham, Honoria Glossop, Soapy Molloy among others – were heard of again. Plum's magic with words and craftsmanship in constructing a story never deserted him, but, inevitably, after the total tally of his books passed sixty or so, repetition crept in, the humour became more forced and the zest less spontaneous. Not even Jeeves can stand up to nineteen books written about him. Each new book, however, was eagerly snapped up and some Wodehouse gem would always be found in it.

Books of a different kind which Plum wrote during these years and which were of considerable interest, were three volumes of autobiography – *Bring on the Girls, Performing Flea* and *Over Seventy*. The first of these, written in conjunction with Guy Bolton, contains reminiscences of their days together in the theatre. It gives a vivid and light-hearted account of the American theatre scene between the wars with an abundance of good stories (some of them on the tall side) of such legendary characters as Flo Ziegfeld, George Gershwin, Jerome Kern and Irving Berlin.

Performing Flea is the most interesting of the three books. Since leaving Dulwich Plum had carried on a copious correspondence with his great school friend, William Townend. The earliest of his letters to him had been lost, but those since 1920 had been preserved; and when Townend suggested that these might make a good book, Plum jumped at the idea. He had for some time been thinking about writing an autobiography, but had always shied away from it as he had an inherent dislike of talking about himself. But it seemed to him that these letters, extended and edited where necessary, would be ideal for the purpose.

In *Performing Flea* Plum recalls incidents in his life and gives his opinions – usually unexpected and irreverent – on a wide variety of subjects. But the main importance of the book lies in the advice he gave to Townend on the subject of writing. Plum has always been considered by his fellow writers, whether or not they actually like his books, a master of words and a superb literary technician. So advice from him on the technique of story-telling is invaluable to all aspiring writers. At one time Plum had the idea of including in *Performing Flea* the scripts of the Berlin broadcasts so that people could see how harmless they were. The difficulty here was that he no longer had copies of them, the original ones having been given to the special interrogator at the end of the war. His idea was that he would rewrite them from memory, touching up here and there and leaving out what he thought fit. But this was clearly not on. Monitored copies of the broadcasts did exist, and Plum's publishers insisted that, if they were to be included, they must be word for word as delivered. Subsequently copies of the broadcasts were obtained, but Plum was horrified by them. He shuddered at some of the things he had said. Perhaps for the first time he realised what a fearful mistake they had been. He immediately gave up all ideas of including them in *Performing Flea*, and he also destroyed *Camp Notebook*, the book he had written and hoped one day to publish about life in an internment camp. However, for some reason that is not entirely clear, he did include in *Performing Flea* the section of *Camp Notebook* about every day life in Huy, and it might have been better for his reputation if he had not.

Over Seventy, the last of the autobiographical books, was written in response to a commission from an American magazine editor. It is not so much an autobiography as a collection of anecdotes and random thoughts on such subjects as earls, butlers, New York, Shakespeare and literary critics. Jolly and entertaining, it does not tell one much one did not know before.

Chapter 16

*An inimitable international institution and master humorist.
(Tribute to P.G. Wodehouse on his eightieth birthday by a group
of well-known writers).*

I always thought I was about the dullest subject there was.

In 1954 Plum caused a stir in the English press when he took out American citizenship. This surprised him as he attached little importance to it; he merely felt that it would make life more convenient. In a letter at the time he wrote:

*I don't feel it matters a damn which country one belongs
to and that what I really wanted was to be able to travel
abroad without having to get an exit permit and an entrance
permit, plus, I believe, a medical examination.*

In the event Plum never travelled outside America again. One reason for this may be that, as late as 1951, the British government was still refusing to guarantee that he would not be prosecuted if he came to England. It was not until the early 1960s that such a guarantee was given to him.

The Wodehouse menagerie at Remsenburg

In the last twenty years of his life Plum became more and more glued to Remsenburg. There were many things which kept him there, but perhaps the most compelling was the increasing number of pets taken into care. Any stray dog or cat was sure of a home there:

. . . so the score is now one foxhound, two guinea hens, Squeaky (Pekingese) and two kittens, and we are hourly expecting more cats and dogs to arrive. I think the word must have gone round the animal kingdom that if you want a home, just drop in at Basket Neck Lane, where the Wodehouses keep open house.

For the most part Plum had little love for modern ideas and inventions and kept them at a distance. But, surprisingly, he made an exception of television. Like many elderly people with old-fashioned ideas he had sworn he would never have a television set in the house. But in time he did, and became an addict to soap operas, so much so that he couldn't bear to miss them. On one of his visits Malcolm Muggeridge found him very het up because his favourite soap opera had been interrupted in order to show 'a thug called Khruschev' ranting and banging with his shoe at the United Nations.

As he grew older, visits to New York became less frequent; there was little to take him there. Certainly not the theatre. He had no love at all for the new breed of American musical. Of *My Fair Lady*, the great hit at the time, he wrote that it was 'the dullest, lousiest show I have ever seen. Even as *Pygmalion* without Rex Harrison it was pretty bad, but with Rex Harrison it is awful.' Modern plays too were not to his taste. *Venus Observed*, by the poet-dramatist, Christopher Fry, he called 'a bloody thing . . . by an obviously bloody author. I never suffered so much in my life'. Highbrows might have had a love for Plum but it was not reciprocated.

A considerable problem for Plum in old age was finding

congenial reading matter. This was not provided by the classics. Only Shakespeare he continued to read, but even here he had to force himself, and he admitted that the sight of an Agatha Christie would almost certainly divert him. Otherwise poets like Shelley, Keats or Wordsworth had no interest for him; Jane Austen 'bored him stiff', and for Dickens he had only a reluctant admiration. Nearly all modern fiction appalled him. 'Isn't it incredible,' he wrote, 'that you can print in a book nowadays stuff which, when we were young, was found only on the walls of public lavatories?' It seems that, almost entirely, Plum's reading was of pre-war English detective stories. He could not have too many of these. And he was quite prepared to admit that he had a great liking for 'trash', and would readily have applied to himself what had been written of someone else that 'he read more books not worth reading than any man in England'. 'Do you know,' he wrote to Townend, 'I think the greatest gift one can have is enjoying trash. I can take the rottenest mystery story out of the library and enjoy it. So I can always have something to read.'

An experience in old age Plum did not enjoy was the writing of his biography. In the late 1950s Richard Usborne began a comprehensive study of his works, not so much with a biography in mind as a critical analysis. Plum did not enjoy being analysed. In an interview with Alistair Cooke he said: 'It is a rather frightening thing you know. I am sure it is very conscientious and impressive to have someone go into one's stuff like that, but it's rather unsettling. I mean you turn the stuff out, and then public orators begin to declaim and critics analyse . . . well it's unsettling.' Later David Jasen, an American academic, embarked on a full-scale biography. This too Plum found alarming, especially when Mr Jasen subjected him to long inquisitions. In a letter he wrote: 'We had my biographer to lunch on Saturday – his invitation not mine, and he made me sit and talk about myself from 1.30 to 5.30, by which time I was nearly dead. What a ghastly bore it is having to talk about oneself. I always thought I was about the dullest subject there was; but he drinks in my every word, blast him.' Left to himself, Plum would have had nothing to do with a biography, but it seems that Ethel was keen on the idea, and so it went ahead, and Wodehouse devotees must be grateful to Mr Jasen for prising out of Plum details of his life which otherwise might never have come to light.

A more agreeable event for Plum was the celebration of his eightieth birthday. On 14th October 1960 his American publishers took a two-column advertisement in the New York Times, only to find that they were a year too soon, so a quick change had to be made in the wording from Plum's eightieth birthday to his 'entering his eightieth year'. This announcement hailed Plum as 'an inimitable international institution and master humorist' and saluted him with thanks and affection. It was signed by eighty of the most famous living English and American writers including W. H. Auden, John Betjeman, Graham Greene, Evelyn Waugh, Rebecca West, Ogden Nash, James Thurber and Richard Rodgers.

In England the occasion was celebrated in the following year and there were numerous tributes in the press and on the radio, of which the one outstanding was by Evelyn

Waugh. In a broadcast, which was later reprinted in the *Sunday Times*, Waugh first of all made what he called 'an act of homage and reparation'. This consisted of a vigorous defence of the Berlin broadcasts and a hard-hitting attack on the way Plum had been treated at the time. Waugh said that the broadcasts had been heard by a negligible number of people in this country, that they contained no political implication of any kind and that the nearest he came to comforting the enemy was to suggest that they were human beings, neither admirable nor lovable, but human, and that this had been represented as 'kneeling in worship of Hitler'. Waugh concentrated his fire on the journalist, Connor (Cassandra), although he did not mention him by name. Revealing for the first time that the governors of the B.B.C. had been compelled to allow his broadcast against their better judgement, Waugh went on: 'It is, therefore, with great pleasure that I take this opportunity to express the disgust that the B.B.C. has always felt for the injustice of which they were guiltless and their complete repudiation of the charges so ignobly made through their medium.'

Although Waugh's words were well meant, it would probably have been better if they had not been said. They caused Plum considerable distress. The one thing he wanted was for the Berlin broadcasts to be forgotten. He was also worried about the effect they would have on the friendship which had developed between himself and Connor. It had been at his request that Waugh did not mention Connor by name, and before the broadcast had taken place he had written in some anxiety to Connor that Waugh was going to make an attack on him, and

160

wanted him to know that he had had nothing to do with it. With great magnanimity he went on: 'Even before I met you, I had never had any ill-feeling about that B.B.C. talk of yours. All you had to go on was that I had spoken on the German radio, so naturally you let yourself go. And what the hell! It's twenty years ago.' Unfortunately this magnanimity was not reciprocated, and when Waugh's broadcast had been made, Connor felt obliged to return to the attack in the *Daily Mirror* with emotional claptrap about the bombing of London and the extermination of the Jews, and seeming to imply that Plum had somehow condoned these. Whatever one might think of Connor's original broadcast in the heat and fury of war, surely to resurrect the lies and innuendoes twenty years later was unforgivable.

The second part of Evelyn Waugh's broadcast consisted of a warm and exceptionally eloquent appreciation of Plum as a writer:

> *Most of us who rejoice in his work do so primarily for the exquisite felicity of the language. That, it seems, is a minor consideration to the author. Either it comes to him unsought, an inexplicable gift like Nijinsky's famous levitations, or it is a matter on which he is so confident in his own judgement that he does not trouble to mention any hesitations he may experience ... I should say that his exquisite diction, as natural as birdsong, is a case of genuine poetic inspiration. I don't believe Mr Wodehouse knows where it comes from and how; wherever he is, in luxury, or in prison, he is able to sequester himself and, as it were, take dictation from his daemon.*

Waugh also stressed strongly that Plum's characters were creatures of his own imagination and had little to do with real life:

Mr Wodehouse's characters are not, as has been fatuously suggested, survivals of the Edwardian age. They are creations of pure fancy – and I use pure in both its senses. They fall in love impetuously and ardently, these figures of Mr Wodehouse's imagination. Their sole failure of chivalry is the occasional mercenary pursuit of an heiress. Seduction and adultery are unknown among them. But they are capable of most other moral lapses. They fall into rages. They get drunk. They smuggle. They rob. They commit arson. They kidnap. They blackmail. They even resort to violence – quite a number of innocent and guilty alike, even the police, get knocked on the head. Professional criminals abound, but they are not the brutes of recent fiction, still less of real life. There are horrific aunts in plenty, but they are not the aunts of 'Saki' Munro. All, whatever the delinquencies attributed to them, exist in a world of pristine paradisal innocence.

For Mr Wodehouse there has been no fall of man; no 'aboriginal calamity'. His characters have never tasted the forbidden fruit. They are still in Eden. The gardens of Blandings Castle are that original garden from which we are all exiled. The chef Anatole prepares the ambrosia for the immortals of high Olympus. Mr Wodehouse's world can never stale. He will continue to release future generations from captivity that may be more irksome than our own. He has made a world for us to live in and delight in.

Chapter 17

Nature had equipped him with a mind so admirably constructed for withstanding the disagreeableness of life that, if an unpleasant thought entered it, it passed out again a moment later.

His face wore the strained haggard look it looks when he hears that guests are expected for the weekend.

The praise lavished on Plum at the time of his eightieth birthday touched him profoundly and must have done much for his self-confidence. This was never stable. 'I sometimes wonder,' he wrote in his old age, 'if I really am a writer.' And again: 'I feel I've been fooling the public for fifty years.' With burgeoning sales and a stream of praise from eminent men of letters such thoughts might seem extraordinary. But Plum was always liable to take to heart the words of those critics who dismissed his work as light, escapist literature with no social significance and himself as a figure from a bygone age who lived a remote, self-centred life, out of touch with reality. That there is an element of truth in this charge cannot be denied. Plum was an escapist. In private life he was the kindest of men who hated to give pain to anyone, but with the agonies of suffering humanity he did not concern himself. Plum once said that, of all the characters he had created, he himself was most like Lord Emsworth who was certainly an escapist. Perhaps one of the closest insights Plum gave into his own character was when he introduced Lord Emsworth in *Something Fresh*:

> *Other people worried about all sorts of things — strikes, wars, suffragettes, diminishing birth-rates, the growing materialism of the age and a score of similar subjects. Worrying, indeed, seemed to be the twentieth century's speciality. Lord Emsworth never worried. Nature had equipped him with a mind so admirably constructed for withstanding the disagreeableness of life that, if an unpleasant thought entered it, it passed out again a moment later . . .*
>
> *His was a life which lacked, perhaps, the sublimer emotions which raised man to the level of the gods, but it was undeniably an extremely happy one. He never experienced the thrill of ambition fulfilled, but, on the other hand, he never knew the agony of ambition frustrated. His name, when he died, would not live for ever in England's annals; he was spared the pain of worrying about this by the fact that he had no desire to live for ever in England's annals. He was possibly as nearly contented as a human being can be in this century of alarms and excursions.*

To some, Plum's indifference to the outside world was unforgivable, but these stern critics overlook one fundamental point: if Plum's interests and sympathies had not been so narrow, he would not have been the writer he was. If he had been politically minded with a social conscience and a message for mankind, he might, perhaps, have been a better man, but he would have been a lesser writer. One further point his critics might bear in mind is that, unrealistic and frivolous though his writing may be, it nevertheless had considerable influence. Plum, himself, would certainly have been stunned to hear this. He always maintained firmly that his works contained no message or moral and that their only purpose was to entertain. But can there be any doubt that they did more than this? Have not millions been affected by their essential gentleness? And have not millions more been helped to develop that most priceless asset – a sense of humour? Plum may not have intended it but his message is clear: that many of those things which the world holds dear – riches, position, success, cleverness – have a humorous, not to say ridiculous, side. If some of the famous figures of the twentieth century had realised this more clearly, would the history of our times not have been happier?

Inevitably, as he grew older, Plum's health became more precarious. When he was in his early seventies he had a minor stroke while walking down Park Avenue. (He wandered into a nearby doctor's surgery where at first, owing to the extreme tattiness of his clothes, he was mistaken for a down and out.) From then on he began to slow down. Arthritis took a hold on him so that walking, especially up and down stairs, became painful. But he remained completely contented. Malcolm Muggeridge visited him again in 1965 in order to interview him for a B.B.C. television programme – not, as it turned out, a very illuminating one as Plum gave only the briefest of answers. But it did emerge that he was still adhering exactly to his time-honoured routine and was still writing about six hundred words a day.

Increasingly in old age Plum became more of a recluse. He never really wanted to see anyone except Ethel, Guy Bolton and, occasionally, his grandchildren. When strangers arrived he tended to disappear.

Plum died on 14th February 1975, when he was ninety-three. Two months earlier he had been created a Knight Commander of the British Empire, so it can be hoped that he died knowing that his country had forgiven him and, perhaps, had tacitly recognised that he had been more sinned against that sinning. And the torrent of congratulations that poured in from all over the world must have reassured him that he was, indeed, a writer of genius.

P. G. Wodehouse
A Treasury of His Wit

Few labours of love are as great as compiling a Wodehouse Treasury. So many gems are there for the taking. Few writers have been so much quoted and caused so much laughter. They are fascinating too in revealing Wodehouse's tastes and distastes – a liking for stately homes, eccentric aristocrats and life below stairs, and a strong aversion to movie tycoons, muscular young women and formidable older ladies. The quotations are arranged, somewhat arbitrarily, under a wide variety of headings, ranging from clergy to policemen and big game hunting to Olde Englishe Teashoppes. Wodehouse's genius was certainly far-reaching.

Human Conditions and Characteristics

He spoke with a certain what-is-it in his voice, and I could see that, if not actually disgruntled, he was far from being gruntled.

A poor human wreck with one foot in the grave and the other sliding towards it.

Nature had made him essentially a passive organism, and it was his tendency, when he found himself in a sea of troubles, to float plaintively, not to take up arms against it.

Mr Crocker said nothing. Constant practice had made him an adept at saying nothing when his wife was talking.

. . . how baggy his clothes looked; what absurdly shaped shoes he wore; how appalling his hat was; how little hair he had; and how deplorably he lacked all those graces of repose, culture, physical beauty, refinement, dignity and mental alertness which raise men above the level of the common cockroach.

As far as such an action was within the scope of a man weighing 260 lbs Lord Uffenham bridled.

I shouldn't wonder if right from the start Mrs Bingo hasn't had a sort of sneaking regret that Bingo isn't one of those strong, curt, Empire-building kind of Englishman she puts into her books, with sad, unfathomable eyes, lean, sensitive hands and riding boots.

Perhaps the greatest hardship in being an invalid is the fact that people come and see you and keep your spirits up.

Nature has so arranged it that in no circumstances could Percy Pilbeam's face ever become really beautiful; but at this moment there stole into it an expression which did something to relieve, to a certain extent, its normal unpleasantness. It was an expression of rapture, of joy, of almost beatific happiness – the look, in short, of a man who sees his way clear to laying his hands on five hundred pounds.

An ape in more or less human form.

He looked like something that had just been prepared for stuffing by a taxidermist.

When he saw me, his mouth sort of flickered at one corner, which I took to be his idea of smiling, and he said 'Ha, young man!' Not particularly chummily, but he said it; and my view was that it practically amounted to the lion laying down with the lamb.

Major Plank relapsed into a sandbagged silence.

She had the appearance of a woman who has been taking aspirins and bathing her temples with eau-de-Cologne.

Take him for all in all, Mr Nickerson looked like one of the less amiable prophets of the Old Testament about to interview the captive monarch of the Amalekites.

She had red hair and the nature which generally goes with red hair. She was impulsive and quick of tongue, and a little too ready for combat.

Something of his former Gawd-help-us-ness seemed to return to him.

His manner became portentous. He looked like Hamlet's father's ghost about to impart a fearful tale.

Old Lady Punter had gone up to her boudoir with a digestive tablet and a sex novel.

He belonged to the school of thought which holds that if you talk quick the words will take care of themselves.

He possessed the art of saying the obvious in a number of different ways to a degree which is found usually only in politicians.

His bearing was so courteous, his manner so reverent that Mrs Stubbs, who had come in like a lioness, began to envisage the possibility of going out like a lamb.

He was a stout, round, bald, pursy little man of about fifty, who might have been taken for a Silver Ring bookie or a minor Shakespearian actor and, oddly enough, in the course of a life in which he had played many parts, he had actually been both.

It is never difficult to distinguish between a Scotsman with a grievance and a ray of sunshine.

'This,' he said, 'is like being in heaven without going to all the bother and expense of dying.'

Augustus Robb – a snob from the crown of his thinly-covered head to the soles of his substantial feet.

The Aristocracy

One of the hottest earls who ever donned a coronet.

The Hon. Galahad had heard the chimes at midnight. And when he had looked in at the old Gardenia, commissionaires had fought for the privilege of throwing him out.

A simple soul, Lord Marshmoreton – mild and pleasant. Yet put him among the thrips, and he became a dealer-out of death and slaughter, a destroyer in the class of Attila the Hun and Genghis Khan. Thrips feed on the underside of rose leaves, sucking their juice and causing them to turn yellow; and Lord Marshmoreton's views on these things were so rigid that he would have poured whale-oil solution on his grandmother if he had found her on the underside of one of his rose leaves sucking its juice.

A writer, describing Blandings Castle in a magazine article, had once said: 'Tiny mosses have grown in the cavities of the stone, until, viewed near at hand, the place seems shaggy with vegetation.' It would not have been a bad description of the proprietor. Fifty-odd years of serene and unruffled placidity had given Lord Emsworth a curiously moss-covered look.

Gally was one of the nibs, one of the lights of London, one of the great figures at whom the world of the stage, the racecourse, and the rowdier restaurants pointed with pride.

If the ruling classes of the island kingdom have a fault, it is that they are inclined when at table to sit champing their food in a glassy-eyed silence, doing nothing to promote a feast of reason and a flow of soul.

When a young man of shy disposition, accustomed to the more Bohemian society of Chelsea, finds himself alone on her home ground with a daughter of a hundred earls and cannot forget that at their last meeting he mistook her for the cook and tipped her half a crown . . . it is almost too much to expect that the conversation will proceed from the first with an easy flow.

Unlike the male codfish which, suddenly finding itself the parent of three million five hundred thousand little codfish, and cheerfully resolves to love them all, the British aristocracy is apt to look with a somewhat jaundiced eye on its younger sons.

An obsolete relic of an exploded feudal system.

Reluctant though one may be to admit it the entire British aristocracy is seamed and honeycombed with immorality.

The floor was crowded with all that was best and noblest in the county; so that a half-brick, hurled at any given moment, must infallibly have spilt blue blood. Peers stepped on the toes of knights; honourables bumped into the spines of baronets. Probably the only titled person in the whole of the surrounding country who was not playing his part in the glittering scene was Lord Marshmoreton; who, on discovering that his private study had been converted into a cloakroom, had retired to bed with a pipe and a copy of *Roses Red and Roses White* by Emily Ann Mackintosh, which he was to discover – after he was between the sheets, and it was too late to repair the error – was not, as he supposed, a treatise on his favourite hobby, but a novel of stearine sentimentality dealing with the adventures of a pure young English girl and an artist named Claude.

We may say what we will against the aristocracy of England, but we cannot deny that in certain crises blood will tell. An English peer of the right sort can be bored nearer to the point where mortification sets in, without showing it, than any other person in the world.

These times in which we live are not good times for earls. Theirs was a great racket while it lasted, but the boom days are over. A scattered few may still have a pittance, but the majority, after they have paid their income tax and their land tax and all their other taxes, and invested in one or two of the get-rich-quick schemes thrown together for their benefit by bright-eyed gentlemen in the City, are generally pretty close to the bread line.

'Even in the post-war days,' said Bill Rowcester, 'with the social revolution turning handsprings on every side and civilisation in the melting-pot, it's still quite an advantage to be in big print in *Debrett's Peerage*.'

Alcohol and its Effects

When I was a bachelor it was rather a habit of mine to get a trifle submerged on occasions of decent mirth and festivity.

Gussie got lit up like a candelabrium.

Dear old Squiffy was always rather a lad for the wassail-bowl. When I met him in Paris, I remember, he was quite tolerably blotto.

Stewed to the gills.

Fried to the tonsils.

Stewed to the eyebrows.

Vastly different was the Gussie who stood before me now. Self-confidence seemed to ooze from the fellow's every pore. His face was flushed, there was a jovial light in his eyes, the lips were parted in a swashbuckling smile. And when with a genial hand he sloshed me on the back before I could sidestep, it was as if I had been kicked by a mule.

I have a headache that starts at the soles of my feet and gets worse all the way up.

. . . and then some invisible person would meanly insert a red-hot corkscrew in the top of his head and begin to twist it.

Social Distinctions

What a curse these social distinctions are. They ought to be abolished. I remember saying that to Karl Marx once, and he thought there might be an idea for a book in it.

There is no anguish so acute as that experienced by a woman of strong views on class distinction, who, having lavished all the charm of her best manner on a supposed scion of the nobility, discovers he is the latest addition to her domestic staff.

Physical Traits

An enormous mass of a man with a squashed nose and ears like the handles of an old Greek vase.

Already a second edition of his chin had been published.

. . . the eyes glaring, the moustache bristling and the *tout ensemble* presenting a strong resemblance to a short-tempered tiger of the jungle which has just seen its peasant shin up a tree.

He wore a little moustache, which to George's prejudiced eye seemed more a complaint than a moustache.

The little man in the sack suit smiled a genial smile, revealing in the process a set of teeth of that perfect whiteness and regularity which Nature can never produce and only the hand of the artist is able to achieve.

For as plainly as if he had carried a sign, this man wore the word 'plug-ugly' written all over him.

Have you ever seen Spode eat asparagus? Revolting. It alters one's whole conception of Man as Nature's last word.

She fitted into my biggest armchair as if it had been built round her by someone who knew they were wearing armchairs tight about the hips that season.

179

Tight fit in an armchair

. . . the manners of a bear aroused while hibernating.

He had small, bright eyes and a sharply curving nose. He looked much more like a parrot than most parrots do. It gave strangers a momentary shock of surprise when they saw Bream Mortimer in restaurants, eating roast beef. They had the feeling that he would have preferred sunflower seeds.

A sharp roar which would have been noticeably stentorian in a sea captain exchanging remarks with one of his men who happened at the moment to be working in the crow's nest.

In shape, he resembled a pear, reasonably narrow at the top but getting wider and wider all the way down and culminating in a pair of boots of the outsize or violin-case type. Above these great, spreading steppes of a body there was poised a large and egg-like head, the bald dome of which rose like some proud mountain peak from a foothill fringe of straggling hair.

He had an enormous bald head, all the hair which ought to be on it seeming to have run into his eyebrows, and his eyes go through you like a couple of death rays.

As he sat there in conference with his wife's sister Mabel, his brow was furrowed, his eyes bulged, and each of his three chins seemed to compete with the others in activity of movement.

The motion-picture magnate, already mauve, turned a royal purple.

He observed that the young man's knotted and combined locks had parted and that each particular hair now stood on end like quills upon the fretful porpentine.

The Right Hon. was a tubby little chap who looked as if he had been poured into his clothes and had forgotten to say 'when!'

Tuppy has one of those high squeaky voices that sound like the tenor of the village choir failing to hit a high note.

The Clergy

... the Rev. P. P. Briscoe who vetted the souls of the local peasantry at a place called Maiden Eggesford down in Somersetshire.

Golly! When you admonish a congregation, it stays admonished.

The Bishop of Stortford was talking to the local Master of Hounds about the difficulty he had in keeping his vicars off the incense.

A tall, drooping man, looking as if he had been stuffed in a hurry by an incompetent taxidermist, it became apparent immediately that he was not one of those boisterous vicars who, when opening a village concert, bound on the stage with a whoop and a holler, give the parishioners a huge hello, slam across a couple of travelling-salesmen-and-farmer's daughter stories and bound off beaming.

The Divine Emotion

A rose-coloured mist swam before his eyes. Piccadilly before he had found flat and uninteresting. Now it was a golden street in the City of Romance, a main thoroughfare of Baghdad, one of the principal arteries of the capital of Fairyland.

She makes me yearn to be a better, nobler, deeper, broader man.

'Bertie,' said Tuppy, now becoming purely ga-ga, 'I may as well tell you that I'm in love at last. This is the real thing. I have found my mate. All my life I have dreamed of meeting some sweet, open-air girl with all the glory of the English countryside in her eyes, and I have found her.'

She turned for an instant to Bingo and there was a look in her eyes that one of those damsels in distress might have given the knight as he shot his cuffs and turned away from the dead dragon.

I dream all the time of some sweet girl who will some day come into my life like a tender goddess and gaze into my eyes and put a hand on each cheek and draw my face down to hers and whisper: 'My man!'

What bungs a fellow over with a refined and poetical girl is soul.

And the more he looked at her, the more he felt a lifetime spent in gazing at Elizabeth Bottsworth would be a lifetime dashed well spent.

Though he scorned and loathed her, he was annoyed to discover that he loved her still. He would have liked to bounce a brick on Prudence Whittaker's head, and yet, at the same time, he would have liked – rather better, as a matter of fact – to crush her to him and cover her face with burning kisses. The whole situation was very complex.

He had just seated himself in the empty waiting room and was turning the pages of a three-months' old copy of *The Tatler* when the door opened and there entered a girl at the sight of whom something seemed to explode on the left side of his chest like a bomb. *The Tatler* swam before his eyes, and when it solidified again he realised that love had come to him at last.

What I mean is, she makes me feel alert and dashing, like a knight-errant or something of that kind.

She paused and heaved a sigh that seemed to come straight up from the cami-knickers.

In a situation calling for words of molten passion of a nature calculated to go through Madeline Bassett like a red-hot gimlet through half a pound of butter, he had said not a syllable that could bring a blush to the cheek of modesty, merely delivering a well-phrased but, in the circumstances, quite misplaced lecture on newts.

That wonder girl in whose half-pint person were combined all the lovely qualities of woman of which he had so often dreamed beneath full moons or when the music of the wind came sighing through the pines, or, for the matter of that, when the band was playing Träumerei.

She flung herself on her husband's ample bosom, sniffing emotionally. Nothing marred the ecstasy of this supreme moment, except those pangs of remorse which still continued to rend her. 'Sap,' she was feeling, was the exact word. She must have been a super-sap not to have understood from the start that her Soapy would never have dreamed of bestowing caresses upon another woman, unless actuated by the soundest commercial motives.

Presently the long, tender embrace ended. Mr Molloy said 'Gee!' and lit a cigar. Mrs Molloy said 'Gosh' and powdered her nose. They walked along together in silent contentment. 'Oh, blessings on the falling out that all the more endears,' they were possibly saying to themselves. Or possibly not.

Have you seen her sideways, Bertie? That cold, pure profile. It just takes all the heart out of one.

Dudley Pickering was not a self-starter in the motordrome of love. He needed cranking.

He sighed as well as he could with his mouth full of cutlet.

His love had burned steadily, a strong silent passion of such a calibre that sometimes, as he sat listening to the hyenas and gazing at the snows of Kilimanjaro, it had brought him within an ace of writing poetry.

It's curious how, when you're in love, you yearn to go about doing acts of kindness to everybody. I am bursting with a sort of yeasty benevolence these days, like one of those chaps in Dickens. I very nearly bought you a tie in London, Bertie.

As a child of eight Mr Trout had once kissed a girl of six under the mistletoe at a Christmas party, but then his sex life had come to an abrupt halt.

He was conscious, as was his custom in her presence, of a warm, prickly sensation in the small of the back. Some kind of elephantiasis seemed to have attacked his hands and feet, swelling them to enormous proportions. He wished profoundly that he could get rid of his habit of yelping with nervous laughter whenever he encountered the girl of his dreams. It was calculated to give her the wrong impression of a chap – make her think him a fearful chump and whatnot!

How strange it is that the great emotional scenes of history, one of which is coming along almost immediately, always begin in this prosaic way. Shakespeare tries to conceal the fact, but there can be little doubt that Romeo and Juliet edged into their balcony scene with a few remarks on the pleasantness of the morning.

'. . . I'm not fond of girls as a rule.' 'Oh, aren't you?'
    'No!' said Sam decidedly. It was a point which he wished to make clear at the outset. 'Not at all fond. My friends have often remarked upon it. A palmist once told me that I had one of those rare spiritual natures which cannot be satisfied with substitutes but must seek and seek till they find their soul-mate. When other men all around me were frittering away their emotions in idle flirtations which did not touch their deeper natures, I was . . . I was . . . well, I wasn't, if you see what I mean.'

A curious happiness pervaded his entire being. He felt young and active. Everything was emphatically for the best in this best of all possible worlds. The sun was shining. Even the sound of someone in the street below whistling was pleasant to his ears, and this in spite of the fact that the unseen whistler only touched the key in odd spots and had a poor memory for tunes.

Archibald, sighting her, reeled as if the cocktail he had just consumed had been his tenth instead of his first.

When I look into those clear, soulful eyes or see that perfect profile bobbing about on the horizon, a sense of my unworthiness seems to slosh me amidships like some blunt instrument. My tongue gets entangled with my front teeth and all I can do is stand there feeling like a piece of Gorgonzola that has been condemned by the local sanitary inspector.

States of Mind

He was not a young man who often had brain-waves, and when they came, they made him rather dizzy.

J. B. Duff did not get ideas; he got obsessions.

His was a slow mind, and you could almost hear it creaking as it worked.

Lord Emsworth had one of those minds capable of accommodating but one thought at a time – if that.

He felt like a man who, chasing rainbows, has had one of them suddenly turn and bite him in the leg.

A wide-eyed gaping gaze, speaking eloquently of a mind imperfectly adjusted to the intellectual pressure of the conversation.

Foggy between the ears.

His demeanour was that of an Assyrian who, having come down like a wolf on the fold, had found in residence not lambs but wild cats, than which, of course, nothing makes an Assyrian feel sillier.

Joy had made him the friend of all the world. He was more like something out of Dickens than anything human.

Cyril blew in, full of good cheer and blitheringness.

Madder than a bull-pup entangled in a fly-paper.

His IQ is about thirty points lower than that of a not too agile-minded jellyfish.

Golf

The least thing upsets him on the links. He misses short putts because of the uproar of the butterflies in the adjoining meadows.

When I played, I never lost my temper. Sometimes, it is true, I may, after missing a shot, have broken my club across my knees; but I did it in a calm and judicial spirit, because the club was obviously no good and I was going to get another one anyway.

Morality and its Absence

'It's an unpleasant thing to say about anyone,' he said, 'but the fact of the matter is that Gertrude's the soul of honour. I believe it comes from playing hockey.'

His conscience, if he had ever had one, had become atrophied through long disuse.

The sensational criminality of the suggestion just made to him awoke no horror in Mr Carmody's ample bosom. He was startled, as many men might be who had this sort of idea sprung suddenly on him in his own garden, but he was not shocked. A youth and middle age spent on the London Stock Exchange had left Lester Carmody singularly broad-minded. He had to a remarkable degree that spacious charity which allows a man to look indulgently on any financial project, however fishy, provided he can see a bit in it for himself.

A woman who with her educated fingers could keep herself in gloves, handkerchiefs, scent, vanity bags and even jewellery free of expense.

G. Ellery Cobbold, that stout economic royalist, had come to his downtown office, all set to prise another wad of currency out of the common people.

Dora Molloy – Fainting Dolly to her friends – was

unquestionably an artist in her particular brand of industry. It was her practice to swoon in the arms of rich-looking strangers in the public streets and pick their pockets as they bent to render her assistance. It takes all sorts to do the world's work.

His was not a high code of ethics ... indeed, in the course of a chequered career he had frequently been guilty of actions which would have caused a three-card-trick man to purse his lips and shake his head.

Similes

A fruity voice like old tawny port made audible.

A sound like two or three pigs feeding rather noisily in the middle of a thunderstorm interrupted his meditations ... The man in the corner went on snoring.

He looked like the hero of a Russian novel debating the advisability of murdering a few more relations before hanging himself in the barn.

As ugly a devil as you would wish to see outside the House of Commons.

The secretary smirked, as Virgil might have done had Dante essayed a mild pleasantry while he was conducting him through the Inferno.

. . . had caused Uncle Tom, who always looked a bit like a pterodactyl with a secret sorrow, to take on a deeper melancholy.

He looked like a rainy Sunday in Pittsburgh.

A tenor voice that sounded like a swooning mosquito.

As bald as a toad's stomach.

. . . an ecstatic expression rather like that of a cherub or seraph on the point of singing Hosanna.

. . . who tended to speak to everyone like a bosun addressing an able-bodied seaman in the middle of a hurricane.

His soul was seething in rebellion like a cistern struck by a thunderbolt.

He looked like a gorilla which had bitten into a bad coconut.

She looked like something that might have occurred to Ibsen in one of his less frivolous moments.

He spoke in a throaty growl, like a Bengal tiger snarling over its breakfast coolie.

He looked like a sheep with a secret sorrow.

He groaned slightly and winced, like Prometheus watching his vulture dropping in for lunch.

Bingo uttered a stricken woofle like a bulldog that has been refused cake.

He looked like a bookmaker who won billiard tournaments.

As slippery as an eel dipped in butter.

Mr Pott disappeared feet foremost, like a used gladiator being cleared away from the arena.

I turned him down like a bedspread.

He, too, seemed disinclined for chit-chat. We stood for some moments like a couple of Trappist monks who have run into each other by chance at the dog races.

Suddenly he shot up like a Young Hindu fakir with a sensitive skin making acquaintance with his first bed of spikes.

A mocking, tinkling laugh which in certain circumstances can churn a man up as if an egg whisk had been introduced into his vitals.

Captain Bradbury hopped into his two-seater like a performing elephant alighting on an upturned barrel.

. . . gave a sort of gurgling scream not unlike a coloratura soprano choking on a fishbone.

As hard-boiled as a fashion plate.

Sir Herbert leaped like a harpooned whale.

Her face was shining like the seat of a bus-driver's trousers.

Some people are made incompatible like film stars and their husbands.

Chivalry

There are times when a man has to forget his chivalry and talk turkey to the other sex. His ancestor, the Sieur Pharamond, had realised this when, returning home from the Crusades rather earlier than had been expected, he found his wife in her boudoir singing in close harmony with three troubadours.

Family Feelings

As he bowled along in his cab, and reflected that a really charming girl, not in the chorus of any West End theatre, a girl with plenty of money and excellent breeding had – in a moment, doubtless, of mental aberration – become engaged to be married to his son, he told himself that life was at last absolutely without a crumpled rose leaf.

The return of the Crusader

Colonel Wedge had supposed himself to be alone with Nature. The shock of discovering that what he had taken for a pile of old clothes was alive and a relation by marriage caused him to speak a little sharply.

I have the highest esteem for Aunt Dahlia, and have never wavered in my cordial appreciation of her humanity, sporting qualities and general good-eggishness.

Years before, and romantic as most boys are, his lordship had sometimes regretted that the Emsworths, though an ancient clan, did not possess a Family Curse. How little he had suspected that he was shortly, to become the father of it.

Laughter

Mr Slattery rumbled like a semi-extinct volcano. It seemed to be his way of expressing amusement.

Her laugh was like a steam-riveting machine.

A sort of writhing movement behind his moustache showed that Sir Aylmer was smiling.

Madeline Bassett laughed the tinkling, silvery laugh which was one of the things that had got her so disliked by the better element.

Aunt Dahlia guffawed more liberally than I had ever heard a woman guffaw. If there had been an aisle, she would have rolled in it ... She was giving the impression of a hyena which had just heard a good one from another hyena.

She had a penetrating sort of laugh. Rather like a train going into a tunnel.

Lottie Blossom had a happy nature, and her lungs were good. When she laughed, she laughed.

The Seaside

When Sam Marlowe reached England he was indeed a soul in torment. Black thoughts obsessed him, so much so that he felt he must have a period of solitude, preferably in the most depressing place he knew. And he had little doubt where this was. Bingley-on-Sea would suit his mood exactly. Here it was grey and dark, and it rained all the time, and the sea slunk about in the distance like some baffled beast.

Bridmouth-on-Sea is notorious for its invigorating air. Corpses at Bridmouth-on-Sea leap from their biers and dance around the maypole.

Rugby Football

Rugby football is a game I can't claim absolutely to understand in all its niceties, if you know what I mean. I can follow the broad, general principles, of course. I mean to say, I know that the main scheme is to work the ball down the field somehow and deposit it over the line at the other end, and that, in order to squelch this programme, each side is allowed to put in a certain amount of assault and battery and to do things to its fellow man which, if done elsewhere, would result in fourteen days without the option, coupled with some strong remarks from the bench. But there I stop. What you might call the science of the thing is to Bertram Wooster a sealed book.

Entertainment

Because the way I intend to sing the song I intend to sing will prove to her that there are great deeps in my nature, whose existence she has not suspected. She will see that rough, unlettered audience wiping the tears out of its bally eyes and she will say to herself, 'What ho! The old egg really has a soul!' For it is not one of your mouldy, comic songs, Bertie. No low buffoonery of that sort for me. It is all about angels being lonely and what not . . .

I uttered a sharp cry.

'You don't mean you're going to sing Sonny Boy?'

'I jolly well do.'

He got through the song somehow and limped off amidst roars of silence from the audience.

Formidable Ladies

One of those robust, dynamic girls with the muscles of a welterweight and a laugh like a squadron of cavalry charging over a tin bridge.

The mental outlook of Lady Emily Finch was that of a strong-minded mule, an animal which she resembled in feature as well as temperament.

She expected people to carry out her wishes, and those who knew what was good for them invariably did so.

It was a woman's voice, a quiet, steely voice, a voice it seemed to me, that suggested cold eyes, a beaky nose and hair like gun metal.

For years she had been moving in a world of men who frisked obsequiously about her and curled up like carbon paper if she spoke crossly to them, and she had become surfeited with male worship.

I love her with a devotion which defies human speech, but if you were to place before me the alternative of disregarding her lightest behest and walking up to a traffic cop and socking him on the maxillary bones, you would find me choosing the cop every time.

Miss Peavey often had this effect on the less soulful type of men, especially in the mornings, when such men are not at their strongest and best. When she came into the breakfast-room of a country house, brave men who had been up a bit late the night before quailed and tried to hide behind newspapers. She was the sort of woman who tells a man who is propping his eyes open with his fingers and endeavouring to correct a headache with strong tea, that she was up at six watching the dew fade off the grass and didn't he think that those wisps of morning mist were the elves' bridal veils.

Aesthetically, he admired Lady Constance's appearance, but he could not conceal from himself that in the peculiar circumstances he would have preferred something more fragile and drooping. Lady Constance conveyed the impression that anybody who had the choice between stealing anything from her and stirring up a nest of hornets with a short walking stick would do well to choose the hornets.

. . . a female Trappist monk on one of her more taciturn mornings.

She was a large woman with a fine figure and bold and compelling eyes, and her personality crashed disturbingly into the quiet atmosphere of the room.

She smiled in a steely sort of way, like one of those women in the Old Testament who used to go about driving spikes into people's heads.

. . . something formidable in her face, a touch of that majestic inaccessibility which used to cramp the style of diffident young shepherds in their relations with the more dignified of the goddesses of Mount Olympus.

She looked like a vicar's daughter who plays hockey and ticks off the villagers when they want to marry their deceased wives' sister.

Gloria Salt was tall and slim and the last word in languorous elegance. Though capable of pasting a golf ball two hundred yards and creating, when serving at tennis, the impression that it was raining thunderbolts, her dark beauty made her look like a serpent of Old Nile. A nervous host, encountering her on the way to dine, might have been excused for wondering whether to offer her a dry Martini or an asp.

There are many ways of saying 'Well!' The speaker who had the floor at the moment said it rather in the manner of the prudish queen of a monarch of Babylon who has happened to wander into the banqueting hall just as the Babylonian orgy is beginning to go nicely.

Prudish queen and Babylonian orgy

Stately Homes

In the Middle Ages, during that stormy period of England's history when walls were built six feet thick and a window was not so much a window as a handy place for pouring molten lead on the heads of visitors, Blandings had been an impenetrable fortress.

Before him, a symmetrical mass of grey stone and green ivy, Belpher Castle towered against a light blue sky. On either side rolling parkland spread as far as the eye could see, carpeted here and there with violets, dotted with great oaks and ashes and Spanish chestnuts, orderly, peaceful and English. Nearer, on his left, were rose gardens, in the centre of which, tilted at a sharp angle, appeared the seat of a pair of corduroy trousers, whose wearer seemed to be engaged in hunting for snails. Thrushes sang in the green shrubberies; rooks cawed in the elms. Somewhere in the distance sounded the tinkle of sheep bells and the lowing of cows.

Smattering Hall was one of those vast edifices, so common throughout the countryside of England, whose original founders seem to have budgeted for families of twenty-five or so and a domestic staff of not less than a hundred. 'Home isn't home,' one can picture them saying to themselves, 'unless you have plenty of elbow room.' And so this huge, majestic pile had come into being. Romantic persons confronted with it, thought of knights in armour riding forth to the Crusades. More earthly individuals felt that it must cost a packet to keep up.

In the days before the Welshman began to expand his surplus energy in playing Rugby football he was accustomed, whenever the monotony of his everyday life began to oppress him, to collect a few friends, and make raids across the border into England, to the huge discomfort of the dwellers on the other side. It was to cope with this habit that Dreever Castle, in Shropshire, came into existence. It met a long-felt want. In time of trouble it became a haven of refuge. From all sides people poured into it, emerging cautiously when the marauders had disappeared.

Anger

Colonel Wedge clenched his teeth. A weaker man might have gnashed them.

His companion was looking like a gorilla of testy and impatient habit from whom the keeper is withholding a banana. It would not have surprised Freddy greatly if he had suddenly started drumming on his chest with clenched fists.

'Sheep?' said Bill.
    'Sheep', said Sir Aylmer firmly. 'A poor, spineless sheep who can't say boo to a goose.'
    A more practised debater would have turned this charge

to his advantage by challenging the speaker to name three sheep who could say boo to a goose, but Bill merely stood rigid, his fists clenched, his nostrils dilated, his face mantled with the blush of shame and indignation, regretting that ties of blood and his companion's advanced years rendered impossible that slosh in the eye for which the other seemed to him to be asking, nay pleading, with his every word.

His eyebrows met across the top of his nose, his chin was sticking out from ten to fourteen inches, and he stood there flexing the muscles of his arms, making the while a low sound like the rumbling of an only partially extinct volcano. The impression Freddy received was that at any moment molten lava might issue from the man's mouth, and he wasn't absolutely sure he liked the look of things.

Madder than a bull-pup entangled in fly-paper, he looked like a minor prophet without a beard confronted with the sins of the people, and started in immediately to thunder denunciations.

Butlers

The butler entered the room, a stately procession of one.

Butlers, like clams, hide their emotions well.

Butlers as a class seem to grow less and less like anything

human in proportion to the magnificence of their surroundings. There is a type of butler, employed in the comparatively modest homes of small country gentlemen, who is practically a man and a brother, who hob-nobs with the local tradesmen, sings a good comic song at the village inn, and in times of crisis will even turn to and work the pump when the water supply suddenly fails. The greater the house, the more does the butler diverge from this type. Blandings Castle was one of the more important of England's showplaces, and Beach, accordingly, had acquired a dignified inertia which almost qualified him for inclusion in the vegetable kingdom. He moved, when he moved at all, slowly. He distilled speech with the air of one measuring out drops of some precious drug. His heavy lidded eyes had the fixed expression of a statue.

The butler loomed in the doorway like a dignified cloudbank.

Beach the butler was a man who had made two chins grow where only one had been before, and his waistcoat swelled like the sail of a racing yacht.

He radiated port and pop-eyed dignity. He had splay feet and three chins, and when he walked his curving waistcoat preceded him like the advance guard of some royal procession.

Departures

The hour of departure was near, and there was a good deal of mixed activity going on. Sailors fiddled about with ropes. Junior officers flitted to and fro. White-jacketed stewards wrestled with trunks. Probably the captain, though not visible, was also employed on some useful work of a nautical nature and not wasting his time. Men, women, boxes, rugs, dogs, flowers, and baskets of fruit were flowing on board in a steady stream.

The usual drove of citizens had come to see the travellers off. There were men on the passenger-list who were being seen off by fathers, by mothers, by sisters, by cousins, and by aunts. In the steerage there was an elderly Jewish lady who was being seen off by exactly thirty-seven of her late neighbours in Rivington Street. And two men in the second cabin were being seen off by detectives, surely the crowning compliment a great nation can bestow.

It was the beginning of what the papers call the Holiday Rush. London and its young, like Xenophon's Ten Thousand, were making for the sea.

Teashops

Ye Cosy Nooke, as its name will immediately suggest to those who know their London, is a tea-shop in Bond Street, conducted by distressed gentlewomen. In London, when a gentlewoman becomes distressed – which she seems to do on the slightest provocation – she collects about her two or three other distressed gentlewomen, forming a quorum, and starts a tea-shop in the West End, which she calls Ye Oak Leaf, Ye Olde Willow Pattern, Ye Linden-Tree, or Ye Snug Harbour, according to personal taste. There, dressed in Tyrolese, Japanese, Norwegian, or some other exotic costume, she and her associates administer refreshments of an afternoon with a proud languor calculated to knock the nonsense out of the cheeriest customer.

Physical Fitness

Theoretically, no doubt, the process of exercising flaccid muscles, opening hermetically sealed pores and stirring up a liver which had long supposed itself off the active list ought to engender in a man a jolly sprightliness. In practice, however, this is not always so.

Poetry

I don't want to wrong anybody, so I won't go so far as to say that she actually wrote poetry, but her conversation to my mind, was of a nature calculated to excite the liveliest suspicions.

Rodney Spelvin was in for another attack of poetry . . . He had once been a poet, and a very virulent one, too

... the sort of man who would produce a slim volume of verse bound in squashy mauve leather at the drop of a hat, mostly on the subject of sunsets and pixies.

Poets, as a class, are business men. Shakespeare describes the poet's eye as rolling in a fine frenzy from heaven to earth, from earth to heaven, and giving to airy nothing a local habitation and a name, but in practice you will find that one corner of that eye is generally glued on the royalty returns.

The wastepaper basket was nearly full now, and still his poet's sense told him that he had not achieved perfection. He thought he saw the reason for this. You can't just sit in a chair and expect inspiration to flow – you want to walk about and clutch your hair and snap your fingers.

... the unpleasant, acrid smell of burned poetry.

English Villages

A picturesque settlement, yes. None more so in all Hampshire. It lay embowered, as I believe the expression is, in the midst of smiling fields and leafy woods, hard by a willow-fringed river, and you couldn't have thrown a brick in it without hitting a honeysuckle-covered cottage or beaning an apple-cheeked villager.

Maiden Eggesford, like so many of our rural hamlets, is not at its brightest and best on a Sunday. When you have walked down the main street and looked at the Jubilee Watering Trough, there is nothing much to do except go home and then come out again and walk down the main street once more and take another look at the Jubilee Watering Trough.

Muscular Young Men

At Yale, where he had been educated, Packy Franklyn had been an All-American half-back, but he had tended, he fully realised, rather to undernourish his spiritual self. He had given it the short end, and it was missing, he knew, on several cylinders. He was self-critic enough to be aware that, if there was a department in which he could safely be sold short, it was the department of the soul. How ill it became him, then, not to cooperate to the fullest extent with a girl who was trying to jack it up.

At Eton Stilton had been Captain of the Boats, and he had also rowed assiduously for Oxford. His entire formative years, therefore, as you might say, had been spent in dipping an oar into the water, giving it a shove and hauling it out again. Only a pretty dumb brick would fritter away his golden youth doing that sort of thing – which, in addition to being silly, is also the deuce of a sweat – and Stilton Cheesewright was a pretty dumb brick. A fine figure of a young fellow as far northwards as the neck, but above that solid concrete.

His tastes were simple. As long as he could afford to belong to one or two golf clubs and have something over for those small loans which, in certain of the numerous circles in which he moved, were the inevitable concomitant of popularity, he was satisfied.

He was one of those large, tough, football-playing blokes who lack the more delicate sensibilities . . . Excellent at blocking a punt or walking across an opponent's face in cleated boots, but not so good when it comes to understanding the highly-strung female temperament.

Bill was a splendidly virile young man, and if you had a mad bull you wished dealt with, you could have placed it in no better hands.

No Adonis to begin with, he had been so edited and re-edited during a long and prosperous ring career by the gloved fists of a hundred foes that in affairs of the heart he was obliged to rely exclusively on moral worth and charm of manner.

Courtship

Up to then he had been very much the meek and mild lover, accepting all too readily that Pat could not be expected to look at him when she must know so many other men who were all the things he was not – glib, dashing, suave, men of poise and *savoir faire* who could carry themselves with a swagger. But now John was realising that as well as humility there was also an element of aggressiveness in his make-up – a touch of the demon lover, deriving, perhaps, from some cave man ancestor. And this had a great effect on Pat, indeed she was overwhelmed by it.

A costermonger, sporting with his donah on Hampstead Heath on a Bank Holiday, would probably have felt that Lord Uffenham had the right idea. To Jeff, who since meeting Anne Benedick had become practically pure spirit, his whole technique was appalling. The thought of soiling Anne, that ethereal being, with this knock-'em-down-and-drag-'em-out type of wooing got in amongst his finer feelings as if they had been hit by a black-jack.

With my first young lady we just happened to be sitting in a cemetery, and I asked her how she'd like it to see my name on her tombstone.

Her smile had become a tender benediction. So might a lady of old have smiled on her knight who had proved himself parfait and gentil.

Antipathy

His only thought regarding Mr Plummer was a passionate realisation of the superfluity of his existence.

Take him for all in all he looked like a bit of bad news.

He was brooding on the scene in much the same spirit of captious criticism as that in which Lot had once regarded the Cities of the Plain.

They got on his nerves and stayed there.

From the very start she had felt herself to be in the presence of one whose soul was not attuned to hers. At moments, indeed, only her perfect breeding had restrained her from beating him over the head with the sock which she was knitting for the deserving poor.

Anxiety and Distress

As for Gussie Fink-Nottle, many an experienced undertaker would have been deceived by his appearance and started embalming him on sight.

Outside the birds were singing merrily, and he wished they wouldn't.

He drank coffee with the air of a man who regretted it was not hemlock.

Freddie experienced the sort of abysmal soul-sadness which afflicts one of Tolstoy's peasants when, after putting in a heavy day's work strangling his father, beating his wife, and dropping the baby into the city reservoir, he turns to the cupboard, only to find the vodka bottle empty.

Bill sat down and put his head between his hands. A hollow groan escaped him, and he liked the sound of it and gave another.

Freddie had mooned about with an air of crushed gloom that would have caused comment in Siberia.

Before the end of the second week Archibald had become completely converted to the gospel of the Brotherhood of Man: and, as this made him a graver, deeper Archibald, it was not long, of course, before Aurelia noticed the change. And one night, when they were dancing at the Mottled Earwig, she took him to task in her forthright way, accusing him in set terms of going about the place looking like an uncooked haddock.

Hell, it is well known, has no fury like a woman who wants her tea and can't get it.

He now definitely feared the worst. It was as if he could feel the soup splashing about his ankles.

Modern Writers

The dullest speech I ever heard. The Agee woman told us for three quarters of an hour how she came to write her beastly book, when a single apology was all that was required.

The bold, cold, ruthless novelist in an incence-scented studio

Dark hair fell in a sweep over his forehead. He looked like a man who would write *vers libre*, as indeed he did.

On paper Blair Egglestone was bold, cold and ruthless. Like so many of our younger novelists his whole tone was that of a disillusioned, sardonic philanderer who had drunk the wine cup of illicit love to its dregs, but was always ready to fill up again and have another.

Deprived of his fountain pen, however, Blair was rather timid with women. He had actually never found himself alone in an incense-scented studio with a scantily clad princess reclining on a tiger skin, but in such a situation he would most certainly have taken a chair as near to the door as possible and talked about the weather.

The novelist seemed to bring with him into the room an atmosphere of doom and desolation and despair, of charnel houses and winding sheets and spectral voices wailing in the wind.

Feminine Beauty and the Lack of it

. . . a young woman of stylish appearance and a certain rather bold and challenging beauty. Her golden hair gleamed brassily, her lips were ruddier than the cherry and her eyes sparkling and vivacious.

A lovely girl needs, of course, no jewels but her youth and health and charm, but anybody who had wanted to make Veronica Wedge understand that would have had to work like a beaver.

Her father might look like a walrus and her mother like something starting at a hundred to eight in the two-thirty race at Catterick Bridge, but Hermione herself, tall and dark, with large eyes, a perfect profile and an equally perfect figure, was an Oriental potentate's dream of what the harem needed.

But they were not the sort of eyes that go with a meek and contrite heart, and one doubts if someone like the late John Knox would have taken to her very much.

Bobbie Wickham was a one-girl beauty chorus.

The girl before him was not pretty. She was distinctly plain. Even ugly. She looked as if she might be a stenographer selected for some business magnate by his wife out of a number of competing applicants.

Clothes

It was the largest, most exuberantly ornate specimen of headwear that I had ever seen.

Personally if anyone had told me that a tie like that suited me, I should have risen and struck them on the mazzard, regardless of their age and sex.

People can say what they please about the modern young man believing in nothing nowadays, but there is one thing every right-minded young man believes in, and that is the infallibility of Bodmin's hats. It is one of the eternal verities. Once admit that it is possible for a Bodmin hat not to fit, and you leave the door open for Doubt, Schism, and Chaos generally.

You'd make Solomon in all his glory look like a tramp cyclist.

Nothing in the life of a great city is more complex than the rules that govern the selection of the correct headgear for use in the various divisions of that city. In Bond Street or Piccadilly a grey top hat is *chic*, *de rigueur* and *le dernier cri*. In Valley Fields, less than seven miles distant, it is *outré* and, one might almost say, *farouche*.

The largest most exuberantly ornate specimen of headwear

Animals

Beside him, looking like a Scotch elder rebuking sin, was the Aberdeen terrier Bartholomew.

. . . like a Scotch elder rebuking sin

It is not always a simple matter to gauge the effect of alcohol on a subject unaccustomed to such stimulant. I have known it to have distressing results in the case of parrots ... The late Lord Brancaster owned a parrot to which he was greatly devoted, and one day the bird chanced to be lethargic, and his lordship, with the kindly intention of restoring it to its customary animation, offered it a portion of seed cake steeped in the '84 port. The bird accepted the morsel gratefully and consumed it with every indication of satisfaction. Almost immediately afterwards, however, its manner became markedly feverish. Having bitten his lordship in the thumb and sung part of a sea-chanty, it fell to the bottom of the cage and remained there for a considerable period of time with its legs in the air, unable to move.

She had turned away and was watching a duck out on the lake. It was tucking into weeds, a thing I've never been able to understand anyone wanting to do. Though I suppose, if you face it squarely, they're no worse than spinach.

Any dog will tell you what these prize-ribbon dogs are like. Their heads are so swelled that they have to go into their kennels backwards.

The house was a frothing maelstrom of dumb chums.

The peke followed him. It appeared to have no legs, but to move by faith alone.

The Aberdeen terrier gave me an unpleasant look and said something under his breath in Gaelic.

It looked something like a pen-wiper and something like a hearthrug. A second and keener inspection revealed it as a Pekingese puppy.

Evening

What with all this daylight-saving stuff, we had hit the great open spaces at a moment when the twilight had not yet begun to cheese it in favour of the shades of night. There was a fag-end of sunset still functioning. Stars were beginning to peep out, bats were fooling around, the garden was full of the aroma of those niffy white flowers which only start to put in their heavy work at the end of the day – in short, the glimmering landscape was fading on the sight and all the air held a solemn stillness.

It was one of those still evenings you get in the summer, when you can hear a snail clear its throat a mile away. The sun was sinking over the hills and the gnats were fooling about all over the place, and everything smelled rather topping – what with the falling dew and so on – and I was just beginning to feel a little soothed by the peace of it all . . .

Big Game Hunting

. . . roaming rifle at the ready, the wilder portions of Africa. And she had done it with outstanding success.

You could say what you liked about Clarissa Cork, and a thousand native bearers in their various dialects had said plenty, but you could not deny that she was far-flung and held dominion over palm and pine.

Jane Hubbard was a splendid specimen of bronzed, strapping womanhood. Her whole appearance spoke of the open air and the great wide spaces and all that sort of thing. She was a thoroughly wholesome, manly girl, about the same age as Billie, with a strong chin and an eye that had looked leopards squarely in the face and caused them to withdraw abashed. One could not picture Jane Hubbard flirting lightly at garden parties, but one could picture her very readily arguing with a mutinous native bearer, or with a firm touch putting sweetness and light into the soul of a refractory mule. Boadicea in her girlhood must have been rather like Jane Hubbard.

'She once killed a panther – or a puma, I forget which – with a hat-pin!' said Eustace with enthusiasm.
'I could wish you no better wife!' said Mrs Hignett.

Dancing

As a dancer he closely resembled a Newfoundland puppy trying to run across a field.

He [Jeeves] swings a dashed efficient shoe.

He was a man who never let his left hip know what his right hip was doing.

She said I danced like a dromedary with the staggers.

Policemen

The burly frame, moreover, was clad in a policeman's uniform, and on the feet one noted the regulation official boots or beetle crushers which go to complete the panoply of the awful majesty of the Law.

P.C. Cheesewright arrived on the scene, looking gruesomely official and saying 'What's all this?'

A vast policeman had materialized from nowhere. He stood beside them, a living statue of Vigilant Authority. One thumb rested easily on his broad belt. The fingers of the other hand caressed lightly a moustache that had caused more heart-burnings among the gentler sex than any other two moustaches in C-division. The eyes above the moustache were stern and questioning.

There was a good deal of mud on the policeman's face, but not enough to hide his wounded expression.

Constable Dobbs's was not a face that lent itself readily to any great display of emotion. It looked as if it had been carved out of some hard kind of wood by a sculptor who had studied at a Correspondence Scbool and had got to about Lesson Three.

The sleepless guardian of the peace of King's Deverill was one of those chunky, nobbly officers. It was as though Nature, setting out to assemble him, had said to herself 'I will not skimp.'

He was taut and alert, as became an officer who, after a jog-trot existence of Saturday drunks and failures to abate smoky chimneys, finds himself faced for the first time with crime on a colossal scale.

Violence

He was far too prone to substitute a left hook to the button for that soft answer which the righteous recommend.

Eustace had no objection to danger to the person, provided it was some other person.

Aunts

About the only advantage of having aunts like her is that it makes one travel, thus broadening the mind and enabling one to see new faces.

Her manner was grim and purposeful, the manner of an

aunt who rolls up her sleeves and spits on her hands and prepares to give a nephew the works.

Aunt Dahlia's face grew darker. Hunting, if indulged in regularly over a period of years, is a pastime that seldom fails to lend a fairly deepish tinge to the patient's complexion, and her best friends could not have denied that even at normal times the relative's map tended a little towards the crushed strawberry. But never had I seen it take on so pronounced a richness as now. She looked like a tomato struggling for self-expression.

Aunt Dahlia uttered a cry like a wail of a master of hounds seeing a fox shot.

My Aunt Dahlia has a carrying voice ... If all other sources of income failed, she could make a good living calling the cattle home across the Sands of Dee.

The aunt made a hobby of collecting dry seaweed, which she pressed and pasted in an album. One sometimes thinks that aunts live entirely for pleasure.

Blots on The Escutcheon

Blotsam Castle, a noble pile, is situated at least half a dozen miles from anywhere, and the only time anybody ever succeeded in disgracing the family name, while in residence, was back in the reign of Edward the Confessor, when the then Earl of Blotsam, 'having lured a number of neighbouring landowners into the banqueting hall on the specious pretence of standing them mulled sack, had proceeded to murder one and all with a battleaxe, subsequently cutting their heads off and in rather loud taste, sticking them on spikes along the outer battlements.

This blot on an otherwise (fairly) unstained escutcheon got the family a bad name in the Crusades when, being invited by the Lionheart to come and do his stuff at the Siege of Joppa, he curled up in bed and murmured 'Some other time.'

'God bless my soul!' exclaimed Lord Emsworth, piously commending his safety to heaven, as so many of his rugged ancestors had done on the battlefields of the Middle Ages. He opened the door and slipped through. Blood will tell. An Emsworth had taken cover at Agincourt.

Places of Alcoholic Refreshment

The Beetle and Wedge
The Cow and Caterpillar
The Cow and Wheelbarrow
The Goat and Bottle
The Goat and Grapes
The Goose and Cowslip
The Goose and Gherkin
The Net and Mackerel
The Stitch in Time
The Waggoner's Rest

The Books of P. G. Wodehouse

Doctor Sally
Piccadilly Jim
A Damsel in Distress
A Gentleman of Leisure
Love Among the Chickens
Indiscretions of Archie
Jill the Reckless
The Girl on the Boat
The Adventures of Sally
The Clicking of Cuthbert
The Coming of Bill
The Inimitable Jeeves
Leave it to Psmith
Ukridge
The Heart of a Goof
Carry On, Jeeves
Meet Mr. Mulliner
Money for Nothing
Mr. Mulliner Speaking
Summer Lightning
Very Good, Jeeves
Big Money
If I Were You!
Hot Water
Mulliner Nights
Heavy Weather
Thank You, Jeeves